British Children's Books
in the Twentieth Century

Illustration by Beatrix Potter for
The Tale of Jemima Puddle-Duck
(Warne).

British Children's Books
in the Twentieth Century

Frank Eyre

Longman

LONGMAN GROUP LIMITED LONDON

Associated companies, branches and representatives
throughout the world

Originally published as *20th Century Children's Books* in 1952 for
The British Council by Longmans, Green and Co.
This revised and enlarged edition first published 1971.

ISBN 0 582 15067 1

Printed in Great Britain
by Ebenezer Baylis and Son Ltd.
The Trinity Press, Worcester, and London

Contents

Acknowledgements

The author and publishers gratefully acknowledge permission to reproduce illustrations by the following artists:

Angus and Robertson Ltd. for Norman Lindsay; Ernest Benn Ltd. for Gordon Browne; Basil Blackwell Ltd. for Mary Baker; The Bodley Head Ltd. for Margery Gill, William Stobbs, Fritz Wegner and Rex Whistler; Jonathan Cape Ltd. and the Executrix of the Arthur Ransome Estate for Arthur Ransome; Jonathan Cape Ltd. and Christopher Lofting for Hugh Lofting; Jonathan Cape Ltd. and the artist for John Burningham; Chatto and Windus Ltd. for Helen Bannerman and Robin Jacques; William Collins Sons & Co. Ltd. for Pauline Baynes, Peggy Fortnum, Mary Shepard and Pamela Whitlock; J. M. Dent & Sons Ltd. for Robert Gibbings; Faber and Faber Ltd. for Alan Howard, Richard Kennedy and Leslie Wood; Hamish Hamilton Children's Books Ltd. for Raymond Briggs; William Heinemann Ltd. for Laurian Jones and Helen Oxenbury; Hutchinson Junior Books Ltd. for Dick Hart; Longman Young Books Ltd. for Pauline Baynes, V. H. Drummond, Gareth Floyd, Margaret Horder and Antony Maitland; Macmillan & Co. Ltd. for Brian Wildsmith; Methuen Children's Books Ltd. for Shirley Hughes; Methuen Children's Books Ltd., Maurice Michael and Mrs Maeve Peake for Mervyn Peake; Methuen Children's Books Ltd. and Curtis Brown Ltd. for Ernest Shepard; Frederick Muller Ltd. for Eve Garnett; Oxford University Press for Victor Ambrus, Edward Ardizzone, Susan Einzig, C. Walter Hodges, Charles Keeping, Joan Kiddell-Monroe, William Papas, William Stobbs and Brian Wildsmith; and Frederick Warne & Co. Ltd. for L. Leslie Brooke and Beatrix Potter.

Details of the source of each illustration are given where they appear in the text.

There are three ways of writing for children . . . the third way, which is the only one I could ever use myself, consists in writing a children's story because a children's story is the best art-form for something you have to say.

C. S. Lewis
On Three Ways of Writing for Children

Children are meant to grow up, and not to become Peter Pans. Not to lose innocence and wonder, but to proceed on their appointed journey; that journey upon which it is certainly not better to travel hopefully than to arrive, though we must travel hopefully if we are to arrive. But it is one of the lessons of fairy stories (if we can speak of the lessons of things that do not lecture) that on callow, lumpish and selfish youth, sorrow and the shadow of death can bestow dignity and even sometimes wisdom. . . . Their books, like their clothes, should allow for growth and their books at any rate should encourage it.

J. R. R. Tolkien
Tree and Leaf

Our trust will in the end repose upon masterpieces; upon the great classics of whatever language or literature we are handling. These, in any language, are neither enormous in number, nor extraordinarily difficult to detect, nor (best of all) forbidding to the reader by reason of their difficulty. Upon a selected few of these . . . we may teach at least a surmise of the true delight and, maybe, some measure of taste, whereby our pupil will by an inner guide be warned to choose the better and reject the worse when we turn him loose to read for himself.

Sir Arthur Quiller Couch
On the Art of Reading

Introduction

This is a revised and considerably enlarged edition of a book written in 1950 (but published in 1952) for the British Council's *Arts in Britain* series as an introduction to modern British children's books. The first part of each section of that book consisted of a discussion of publishing developments and their influence on writing for children in the twentieth century, accompanied by analysis of the more significant books. The second part had necessarily to be more speculative, since it dealt with the then contemporary books and an attempt had to be made to discriminate between the good, the bad and the indifferent (the latter usually by exclusion) and to forecast what was likely to survive. It is interesting to find, twenty years later, that no book of real importance was missed and that few of the books discussed are no longer read.

This new edition follows the same general lines, but it should be emphasised that it is more in the nature of an enlargement than, so far as the earlier sections are concerned, a revision. Those parts of the book which deal with the early history of children's books in Britain have been only lightly edited (to clarify a too loose statement, or modify one that now seems dated) and comments on the pre-1950 books have only been revised if subsequent experience with them made re-reading advisable to confirm previous assessments. It seemed more important to concentrate on the addition of new material at the end of each section, to bring the history of writing and publishing for children up to date and to discuss the remarkable number of new books of high quality that have been written in the last twenty years. The final chapter, 'Novels for Young Readers', has been completely re-written.

It is, therefore, now a longer book (necessarily so, since another twenty years' output of children's books had to be considered) but it is hoped that it remains concise and to the point.

The limitations established for the original study have been preserved in this new edition. It is concerned primarily with original work by British writers and artists, and its principal object is to examine the main trends in the development of British children's literature during the first seventy years of this century and to call attention to outstanding books. Although there is rather more discussion in this edition of contemporary trends and their effects on writing and publishing for children, the study is still confined to original imaginative work and no attempt has been made to consider purely informative books, or the many different kinds of 'written for a purpose' books that are now being published.

Nevertheless, the reading undertaken to establish the choice of books discussed has been extensive and continuous over the whole period since the first edition was published. I have been fortunate in that, although after 1950 I was no longer directly involved in publishing books for children, my contact with them in a wider sense has been if anything closer. It has certainly been better informed. Australian children's librarians are energetic, widely read, idealistic and argumentative! Working with them in many ways, on book selection committees, in children's discussion groups, at book weeks, as an officer of children's book councils, I have been constantly exposed to their determination to see that I did my homework. Sixteen years' work with the committee that was responsible for the Victorian Children's Book Council's booklists taught me never to be rash enough to discuss a book in such company unless I had read it properly—all the way through!—and often re-read it if my opinion was hotly disputed, as it frequently was. And it sharpens one's ideas about children's books wonderfully to have growing children of one's own and to be able to talk to them and their friends about the books. Most interesting of all has been the experience (provided by the schools section of the Council) of taking part in discussions with groups of children of many different ages about the books they had read. It would surprise most publishers, and some authors, to hear children's own views of books expressed so freely and so intelligently. Australia has been a good country in which to continue the study of children's books, not only because work on them here is so active and so well organised, but also because the exposure to books from other countries, especially from North America, is so much greater than it is in Britain. It has been enlightening to see British children's books in use under conditions in which they are in direct and constant competition with American ones.

Although there are limitations to this study it is hoped that no really outstanding book has been overlooked, and that adequate attention has been given to new but promising authors. Obviously not all such authors could be mentioned and there must be many not dealt with whose work is likely to be of interest in the future. With 2000 new children's books being published in Britain each year it is impossible for anyone to be certain that he has not missed a promising single book. I have made an honest attempt to read every book that seemed likely to be worth consideration but I have not read every book in every minor series, or every book by every author. Nevertheless I have read at least one, and usually several books by every author who has received critical attention, or whose work has been recommended to me, and all the books of important writers have been read. It should be stressed that failure to mention an author's books does not necessarily mean that they are beneath critical attention. It is more likely to have resulted from a decision that they were in a category that could be adequately dealt with by a general summary of books of the same kind. So much writing for children today is produced to a formula, either to meet a genuine or supposed need or to fit the pattern of either a series or an editor's intentions or wishes, that there are now hundreds of 'mid-quality' books, in consideration of which true critical values rarely count. In discussing these books one will do as well as another and there is little point in attempting to discriminate between them—though many of them may be honestly written and make temporarily satisfying reading.

Those who like to speculate about national character may draw some curious conclusions from this study of the British contribution to modern children's literature. It is notable, for example, that the supposedly stolid British should have produced some of the best of all children's books for that in-between age when fantastic and improbable happenings best hold the dawning mind, and when nothing seems impossible. During the past twenty years the children of this nation of shopkeepers seem to have felt the need for an escape into fantasy—or to the different kind of truth that fantasy offers—and even fiction for older chidren now includes some fine books of this kind. It is noticeable also that when distinguished adult authors write children's books, as they have continued to do during the past twenty years, they are rarely studies of everyday life.

In the same twenty years that part of the contemporary British imagination which has produced this flowering of fantasy has had the same effect on picture books in colour, and the works of Brian Wildsmith, John Burningham, Charles Keeping and other artists have equalled any in the world. It is interesting that these exotic new British books should be so unlike those remarkable North American ones which first introduced a new kind of picture book in the early part of the century. Those were, in the main, didactic, and as often about things as people. There are still few British equivalents of such admirable books as *Mike Mulligan and His Steam Shovel* or *Paddle to the Sea*. Possibly by the time British artists reached sufficient stature this vein had been worked out.

Whatever the cause, these British colour picture books have been of a completely different kind. Brilliant blazes of colour; wild flourishes of imagination; temptations to freedom; keys to open the child's mind to new and undreamt-of worlds —these beautiful books may seem to some adults to serve the artist's purpose rather than the child's, but that semblance is an illusion. Few children can resist them, and those who ask for pictures with a purpose are missing the point. These books form an essential part of a movement in the second half of the twentieth century of British children's books towards a newer and more complete kind of freedom of expression and enjoyment. It is a movement which may in time be reversed but which has given British children the richest harvest of imaginative books of all kinds that any nation has produced.

There are now, in this latter part of the century, apparent trends towards a newer kind of didacticism. 'Purpose' books of various kinds are appearing; the old menace of 'series' books is arising in new forms, often from sincere attempts to produce books that will tempt non-readers to reading. Determined efforts are being made to meet the criticisms so often directed at British children's books—that they are unrealistic and written primarily for and about the children of middle-

class families. It is no longer true to say that there are no
books about real life in difficult circumstances. We have books
about girls with illegitimate children, drunken fathers, and
coloured lovers; about pop stars and back street gangs; about
punch-ups and other violence; about most of the fashionable
topics of today. There are now many such books, some better
than others, but most of them honest in purpose and per-
formance. Nevertheless the majority of them have a slightly
unnatural air. There is a sense of striving, of too deliberate
contrivance, that is missing from other kinds of British children's fiction and it seems likely that this kind of reality does
not come altogether naturally to our writers. This remains, it
seems, a type of book that is done better elsewhere, notably in
North America. But it is possible that new developments in
this type of book may well come from Commonwealth
countries such as Australia whose writers seem to turn to
realism more naturally.

Although I have taken no one's opinion as my own, and
assessed no book without having read it, many people have
guided me to important books. I am specially grateful to
Kathleen Lines, Elaine Moss, Brian Alderson, Edward Blishen,
Naomi Lewis and many others for making suggestions about
the English contribution to this study; to Dorothy Ballantyne
(Neal White) for New Zealand books; to Sheila Egoff for
Canadian books; to Lydia Pienaar for South African books;
and to my friends and colleagues on the Book List Committee
of the Victorian Children's Book Council: Margaret Ingham,
Peggy Young, Maisie Drysdale and many others, who have
for the past sixteen years seen that I continued to read the
best books written for children.

Finally a word should be added about the sections under
which the books have been considered. Children's books are
as difficult to classify as English rivers, which refuse to be
divided tidily into counties or into any recognised regional
groupings. Like the rivers, they overflow their boundaries
and meander through the counties of the mind. Everyone who
takes children's reading seriously has to keep continually in
mind the relationship between the age of the child and the
books he reads, not so much in regard to their suitability—
about which it is impossible to dogmatise—as in relation to a

child's capacity to absorb what he is offered. Innumerable attempts have been made to classify children's books into age levels and in other ways, but they can only be approximations. The problem has grown worse during the last decade, because children are now for many reasons exposed to adult life much earlier. They read the same newspapers and magazines as their parents from the moment they become assured readers, and they look at the same television programmes. The years during which they are prepared to read books specifically designed for children are steadily contracting and, at the same time, because exposure to adult influences affects children of different levels of intelligence and different family backgrounds in widely different ways, the discrepancy between the ages at which different children read the same book has become greater. It is no longer possible to state with any confidence the age at which any children's book beyond the simplest first reading books will be read and this difficulty sharpens at the level at which classification, from the critical point of view, is most useful.

The sections into which this book has been divided are not, therefore, intended to represent rigid classifications and are no more than a convenient method of grouping. The worst difficulties arise in the 'Fiction' section, in which precise classification is made difficult both by variations in reading age and the increasing, but welcome, blurring of the distinctions between, for example, adventure stories and stories of family life, or between school stories and adventure stories. It would be impracticable to abandon these categories without completely re-casting the whole book and they are essential for the examination of the first part of the century, in which such divisions were still sharply apparent. There are also some categories which have continued valid, 'historical novels' for example, and 'fantasy', and one at least, 'school stories', which has staged a remarkable recovery from seeming near-extinction. Such books as *A Swarm in May*, *Seraphina*, or *End of Term* may be worlds away from *The Fifth Form at St Dominic's* but they *are* stories about life at school. Can it be that this is, after all, a form of story that satisfies a continuing need of children?

Although, therefore, continuing to divide the books of the past decade in the same way as those of the previous half-century does present some difficulties (where does one put William Mayne?) the categories have been retained. But to simplify examination of the overall work of a few major writers the whole of their work has been considered in a single section even although it may include books of many different kinds. A new section, 'Novels for Older Children' has also been introduced to deal with borderline books.

Development in children's books is today so fast that it should be stated that the writing of the first draft of this study was completed in March 1970. It has been a long time in the press, but it was as up to date as it could be made when it was written and it is hoped that although some of the authors considered will have written later books nothing has occurred since to make any of its assessments invalid.

Drawing by V. H. Drummond for her book The Flying Postman (*Longman*).

I. Historical Survey

It is not easy to trace the development of children's books in Britain during the past seventy years. It has been a crowded period, complicated by the incidence of two great wars and confused by changes in the social structure and life of the country which, while greatly enlarging the number of readers, have brought new problems to writers, artists and publishers.

Nevertheless some broad lines of development can be discerned, and it is interesting to see how closely these parallel the changing phases in children's publishing during the previous three centuries so ably traced by F. J. Harvey Darton in *Children's Books in England*. From that book two facts emerge clearly. The first is that the history of children's books in Britain cannot be considered apart from the history of publishing, for from the time of the chapmen to the present day the type of children's book made widely available has been governed largely by commercial considerations, and children's books have always been a profitable field not only for the hack writer but also for the hack publisher. This element has been especially prominent in the present century, and since this section is an attempt to analyse the causes of changes in the type of children's book popular throughout the century, it is inevitably concerned to a considerable extent with the problems of publishing.

The second is the fact that it is possible to discern a cyclical pattern in British children's books throughout the centuries, consisting of a continual alternation between the most determinedly moral stories calculated to improve and uplift young readers, and books designed to be read for enjoyment. The former kind of book appears to reign supreme for about half a century, but towards the end a violent reaction begins. Teachers, writers and parents rebel against what they consider to be a suppression of the natural gaiety of children (Charles Lamb took a trenchant part in one such rebellion at the beginning of the nineteenth century) and for the following half-century didacticism is ousted. Children's books become gayer, more natural, and more fun to read. Then the turn of the half-century brings another swing of the pendulum, a swing which curiously enough has more than once derived its initial momentum from the other side of the Atlantic. The kind of person who previously objected to the over-emphasis on morality now begins to plead that 'no one takes children's reading seriously', 'children's books are not informative enough', and before long there is a return to didacticism.

These fluctuations of taste are more violent and more immediately apparent in children's books than in any other form of publishing, for in no other can the public rely on getting so exactly what it wants, and in no other are variations in taste so closely scrutinised or immediately gratified. One successful book produces a host of imitations, and if it is not true that one swallow makes a summer it is certainly true that one Peter Parley produces a hundred.

This alternation between 'what children like' and 'what children ought to have' can be traced throughout the brief history of children's publishing in Britain and is closely related to parallel changes in social thought and behaviour. Thus the Puritan reaction against the alleged licentiousness of the way of life they sought to suppress was paralleled by the introduction of a host of 'goodly' books designed to replace the romances, the *Gesta Romanorum*, the Bestiaries, and the like, which up to that time had been the principal source of reading for children. Similarly the temporary eclipse of fairy tales and nursery rhymes (which superseded the 'goodly' books of the Puritans) by *Sandford and Merton* and the moralities of Mrs Trimmer was equally traceable to changing social conditions—the influence of Rousseau alone on British children's books would make an interesting study.

With each swing of the pendulum, however, the reaction towards didacticism became less pronounced and the books produced became easier to read and enjoy. It is possible, therefore, to see the whole history of British children's publishing as a development towards freedom—freedom of expression, thought, and, above all, of imagination. The idea that a children's book of whatever type ought to have a 'purpose' had by the end of the nineteenth century been over-thrown. *Alice* showed that the imaginative story could exist entirely on its own without purpose or moral; *Treasure Island* did the same for the adventure story; *Stalky & Co.* for the school story; and *A Child's Garden of Verses* for children's verse.

The effects of this revolution were not immediately apparent, for many of the Victorian giants overlapped so prominently into the new century that most people think of them as being later in date than they really are. Kingston, Ballantyne, Mayne Reid, Henty, Fenimore Cooper, Talbot Baines Reed, Mrs Molesworth, and Mrs Ewing, are all writers of the last century, not only in manner but also in date. Even a few long-lived authors such as Frances Hodgson Burnett, whose best book *The Secret Garden* was published in 1910 when she was sixty-five, belong in spirit to the last century and could only by strict interpretation of date be considered as twentieth-century writers. Nevertheless, the movement towards undiluted enjoyment in children's books gradually gained momentum, and if the previous history had been one of a struggle for freedom the history of the present century has been one almost of licence.

The publishing phases of the past seventy years can be con-veniently divided into five periods. The first was from the beginning of the century to the early nineteen-twenties. During that time, although *Treasure Island* and *Stalky & Co.* had led the way to a more natural and lifelike presentation of character and incident in the adventure and school story, other authors were slow to copy them, and for some years the con-ventional type of story by writers like Marryat, Ballantyne, Kingston, Henty, and their latter-day followers, such as Herbert Strang, continued to be popular. But a significant development was the immense increase in popular interest in fairies (which, although producing a few original and dis-tinguished books, also released a spate of trivial and imitative stories) and the new emphasis, which has persisted for the greater part of the period, on fantasy in general. It is notice-able that many of the best books of the period have been of this type, and the present century has also been notable for the number of writers distinguished in other fields who have written books for children. Whatever the reason for this may be, throughout the century famous scholars and scientists, novelists and writers of all kinds have produced books which, whether or not they were originally written for children, have been read by them, and which have, without exception, been fantasies. It is necessary to mention a few only that come to mind to realise the truth of this. A. E. Coppard's *Pink Furniture*, John Masefield's *The Midnight Folk* and *The Box of Delights*, Stella Gibbons's *The Friendly Gnome*, Eric Linklater's *The Wind on the Moon*, Beverley Nichols's *The Stream That Stood Still*, Vaughan Wilkins's *After Bath*, Hilda Lewis's *The Ship That Flew*, T. H. White's *The Sword in the Stone* and *Mistress Masham's Repose*, J. W. Dunne's *The Jumping Lions of Borneo*, Rumer Godden's *The Doll's House*, Professor Haldane's *My Friend Mr Leakey*, Professor Tolkien's *The Hobbit* and *The Lord of the Rings*, Professor C. S. Lewis's *The Lion, The Witch and The Wardrobe*, and Professor W. W. Tarn's *The Treasure of the Isle of Mist*. They make an impressive list, and when it is remembered that three previous examples, Ruskin's *The King of the Golden River*, Dickens's *Captain Boldheart* and Thackeray's *The Rose and the Ring* were also of the same type, one of the main reasons for what is at once the strength and weakness of British children's books becomes apparent. Our writers incline naturally towards works of imagination, whether it be in poetry, drama, or children's books, and there seems almost to be a relation between the quality of a writer and the likelihood of his turning to fantasy when he writes for children. Some possible reasons for this will be examined later. In the meantime the fact need only be noted. Whatever the cause we must be grateful for such a propensity when it produces such results, although it remains disappointing that few adult novelists, when prompted to write children's books, have been prepared to tackle a story of everyday life.

The triumphant return of the fairies in the twentieth century was largely brought about by the overwhelming success of J. M. Barrie's *Peter Pan*. A few years earlier, in 1902, E. Nesbit had published the first of her long series of delightfully natural modern fairy tales, *Five Children—and It*, and with the addition in 1908 of *The Wind in the Willows* by Kenneth Grahame, which brought animal characters into the modern child's dream world of fantasy, the picture was complete. For the remainder of the period authors, artists and publishers devoted their efforts to imitation and little that was not derivative from one or other of these sources appeared.

The publication in 1924 of A. A. Milne's spectacularly successful *When We Were Very Young* coincided with the beginning
of the second phase in twentieth-century children's publishing.
Milne's verses and the stories, *Winnie-the-Pooh* and *The House
at Pooh Corner*, that followed, although they had the inevitable
imitators, were an isolated phenomenon, for the general level
of children's books at this period was very low.

The first twenty years of the century had seen a tremendous
development in the business of publishing for children. It was
a period of expansion, during which the great 'children's
houses' established their reputations and many of the larger
firms formed separate children's departments for the first
time. Many new firms were founded. This development bore
a striking resemblance, although on a much larger scale, to a
similar period of successful children's publishing a hundred
years earlier, immediately after the success of *The Butterfly's
Ball*. Publishers of children's books during that earlier period
prospered through taking advantage of the boom. But in the
nineteen-twenties competition was keener; a number of large
firms were established in a commanding position, and it had
become increasingly difficult for the publisher of an individual
book to compete successfully against the appeal of the
innumerable mass-produced 'series' which were the predominating feature of the period. Just as they were later, but for
different reasons, to become a dominating feature of children's
publishing in the 'sixties.

Soon even the attraction of the 'series' became insufficient,
and about the years 1923–5 'Bumper' books were introduced
to the market. The Bumper book, which it is to be hoped has
not been inflicted on the children of other nations, can be
defined as an attempt to appear to give the best value in the
world while actually offering the worst. The idea, which was
simple enough, was derived from a combination of two prac-
tices, one old, the other new. The first, which had already
begun to desecrate picture books, was the multiple use of
blocks. There was nothing new about *this* practice. Many
publishers of children's books in the middle of the eighteenth
century used the same blocks over and over again without
much regard to their suitability for the text, and Mrs Sher-
wood, the author of *The Fairchild Family*, has recorded that
her publisher used to send her collections of blocks which it
was her 'tedious task to attempt to link with some kind of
story'. But in the twentieth century the practice which may
have begun as a necessity became a deliberate and profitable

policy with many children's publishers. The same blocks were used for innumerable different books and it was not at all uncommon for an unwary parent to take home at Christmas an annual for the family, a story for his six-year-old son, and a picture book for the baby, only to find all three illustrated by the same blocks.

John Newbery proved two hundred years ago that it is perfectly possible to produce profitable children's books without resorting to this practice, and he insisted that no book that he published should be illustrated by blocks that had previously been used for other books. No adult would tolerate such treatment for a moment in the books which he was accustomed to read, and it is sad to reflect that this century, which is in so many ways so enlightened in its treatment of children and its approach to art, should have been responsible not only for such malpractices, but also for a flood of the worst and most tasteless children's picture books ever produced.

The Bumper books were usually made up from stories, illustrations, poems, and so forth, which had appeared in annuals and elsewhere. They were printed from the same type and blocks. Since most of their publishers naturally avoided any material that carried a royalty there were no new capital costs at all, and the Bumper books could therefore be produced very cheaply and gave, by their size and the number of their illustrations, the appearance of being wonderful value. This superficial appearance of value was greatly enhanced by the second feature of the Bumper books, which was the contemporary development of a type of paper known as 'featherweight'. This was first introduced into this country for the Bumper books but soon spread into other fields of children's publishing, with the deplorable result that from about the year 1925 the most important aspect of a children's book became its bulk. The principal feature of featherweight paper is that large quantities of air, which are normally excluded in papermaking, are allowed to remain in the sheet, thus enormously increasing its bulk without adding noticeably to its weight. In consequence, a book of sixty-four pages printed on featherweight looks just as fat as one of two hundred pages on normal paper. Everyone born before 1920 must remember the bulked monstrosities that resulted from the use of this paper for children's books. Apart from the horrible appearance of the books and their very much reduced life (for featherweight paper has insufficient substance to retain adequately the stitching by which a book is held together) the use of this thick paper brought about a still greater reduction in the actual value offered. For what appeared to be a full length story was often actually little more than a short story ingeniously expanded by being printed on featherweight paper in a large type with the lines widely spaced.

By this time children's publishing had become an established and extensive business. The greater part of this business, apart from a few distinguished series of standard classics, was done by a handful of large firms who found their principal market in what was known as the 'Sunday School reward' trade. The intense competition of these firms for such a stolidly conservative market tended to confine the books of the period to an almost rigid uniformity. Anything at all unusual either in content or style of production was suspect, and it became increasingly difficult for the few firms which continued to produce individual children's books of quality to do so at a profit.

It was a period of almost uncontrolled freedom, when anything and everything that might possibly appeal to children was introduced into children's books and when few firms appeared to recognise the wider responsibilities of children's publishing. It was from the books of this period that Noel Carrington and Albert Rutherston were given the task of selecting British children's books for the Paris Exhibition, and Carrington commented: 'We were hard put to it to find a dozen that we could exhibit with national pride. It was borne home on us how many of the best books were fully fifty years old and that too many of the more recent originated in America.'[1]

The most deplorable aspect of this period was the fact that these mass-produced books were not only uninspired, repetitive and boring, but that their ubiquity prevented parents and children from becoming aware of the better class of children's book that had always existed, and so acted as a bar to selection.

In the early nineteen-thirties a new phase opened and the inevitable reaction began. Children's librarians and teachers in the United States had for some years past been studying children's reading and endeavouring to persuade parents and publishers to give more serious attention to the problem. By

[1] Noel Carrington, *Junior Bookshelf*, July 1942.

1930 they had achieved considerable success and the conception that a children's book should do more than merely entertain had become widely accepted. It is noteworthy that the reaction this time was less concerned with morality and more with making children aware of the function and purpose of the material things around them.

Before long the effects began to be felt in Britain, and in the decade before the Second World War several interesting and significant things happened. The Library Association acknowledged work in a children's library as a speciality, and soon after a group of enthusiasts formed a children's librarian section of the Association. Later still an award for the best children's book of the year was established (see p. 177). Many of the smaller and more selective publishing firms were interested in books for children (possibly as a result of the success of A. A. Milne's books) and several of the larger publishers put the management of their children's departments into the hands of professional editors trained in the use of books with children. Eleanor Graham, who had made a great reputation as head of what was probably the most influential children's department of a bookshop in Britain, that of J. and E. Bumpus of Oxford Street, was one of the earliest of these appointments. She exerted considerable influence on the development of children's books in this country, not only as an editor, first at Methuen and later at Penguin, where she established the deservedly successful Puffins (see p. 33), but also as a reviewer and as the writer of several unusual children's books. A similar influence was exerted by Kathleen Lines, a trained children's librarian from the famous Toronto public library, who, in 1938, edited for the National Book Council the first selective classified and annotated list of children's books ever produced in this country. It was simply called *Book List 23*. It did not achieve wide circulation at the time, but after the war it became the foundation for a better-known list, *Four to Fourteen*, which although a completely new list owed its origins to this first conception of the National Book Council.

The movement gathered momentum and before long a platform was found in *The Junior Bookshelf*, the first periodical in Britain exclusively devoted to the critical consideration of children's books. (Its American equivalent, *The Horn Book Magazine* had been established twelve years earlier, in 1924.) The libraries, which had been extremely conservative in their buying, began, as a result of the improved training and greater experience of children's librarians, to exercise a powerful influence in encouraging authors and publishers to produce good children's books. A new and more interesting type of picture book, based largely on successful American models, began to appear, and the publication in 1931 of Arthur Ransome's *Swallows and Amazons* led the way to a new conception of the children's adventure story. It became possible for a book to achieve a modest success without conforming to the standard pattern. It is significant that, although a few of the larger publishing firms had maintained a consistently high standard, many of the best books of the period emanated from publishers who had no 'juvenile' department and produced only occasional children's books.

Illustration by Robert Gibbings for his book Coconut Island (*Dent*).

Unhappily the outbreak of the Second World War put a temporary end to such activities and opened a new phase in twentieth-century publishing for children. That phase witnessed the production of some interesting books in colour, but it was, on the whole, one of intense disappointment to all who are seriously interested in children's reading. For reasons which it would now be unprofitable to examine, a very high proportion of the books which would figure in any list of the best modern children's books were unobtainable during the war years, and far too many inferior books were produced. A contributory factor was, of course, the absence of many authors and artists on war work.

The period served principally to advance the reputation of a few authors who specialised in the mass production of a type of wildly improbable adventure story that for a time became the standard children's fare.

Adventure stories showed little improvement in the years immediately following the war. Criminals of various sorts replaced spies and parachutists, but otherwise the slaughter continued unabated and the majority of adventure stories showed little more imagination or intellectual content than the comic strips. Picture books also declined and the immediate post-war years would have been depressing for those engaged with, or interested in, children's books had it not been for signs that the reaction interrupted by the war was beginning again, this time from our side of the Atlantic. The National Book League encouraged Children's Book Weeks throughout the country and produced the first British full-length classified and annotated list of children's books, *Four to Fourteen* by Kathleen Lines. A new generation of children's editors began to emerge and it slowly became respectable for intelligent adult critics to take a serious interest in books written for children. But efforts at improvement were for a time thwarted by the operation of a children's book variant of Gresham's Law. The commercial success of a type of book allegedly written for children but in fact produced to a formula by cynical opportunists discouraged publishers from risking capital on a different kind of book. Once again the type of book produced for children was being dictated by commercial considerations.

A few publishers continued to produce occasional exceptional books, chosen by editors of quality for reasons which were not purely commercial, but publishers' sales staffs (and accountants) remained resistant to change. To break this barrier two things were needed: a publisher prepared to risk capital on a new kind of children's book list, and intelligent reviewing, reaching a wider public, to make parents aware of the existence of these better books. The introduction in 1949 of a special *Children's Books Supplement* as a periodic feature of *The Times Literary Supplement* was the most encouraging development of this period. Not only because it introduced literate parents to a type of children's book of which many had previously been unaware, but also because it did much to improve the status of the children's writer of integrity, who had in the past to plough a lonely furrow, often with inadequate reward and always without recognition outside a small circle of specialists.

Publishers were finally found willing to risk capital on better books and reviewing continued to improve. By 1950 British children's books were entering a new phase. It is not easy, looking back, to establish just when the change occurred, but it was well on the way at the turn of the half-century. Almost overnight writers who had seemed on a pinnacle of commercial success became disreputable. Their books continued to sell, but at a different level—the steadily increasing population making it possible for their sales to be maintained at this lower level although the majority of educated parents and most libraries ceased to buy them. In their place a new kind of children's book emerged and at the same time a new kind of critic and professionally interested person appeared to admire and write about them. The two developments followed each other so closely that it is difficult now to tell which most influenced the other, but their mutual interdependence is undeniable, for neither could have been so successful without the other.

For the next ten years there was so much good and constructive writing about children's books that the critical situation is now completely transformed. By the 'sixties there were so many good critics that it would be impossible to list them all, but everyone interested in British children's books will acknowledge the pioneer work of such writers as Margery Fisher, whose *Growing Point*, founded in 1962, was the first periodical in this new field of independent critical reviewing for parents rather than librarians (*The Junior Bookshelf* had tended always to be librarian influenced and slanted), and Anne Wood whose *Books for Your Children* was founded in 1965. The intelligent parent who is interested in what his children read no longer has to search for himself or, alternatively, trust blindly to a single opinion. He has a wide range of journals and critics to choose from and can compare one critic's view with another's and form his own opinion, just as he has long been accustomed to do for his own reading, or theatre- or film-going.

The critical journals have come of age, and so have the critics. The writer for children can now confidently expect informed reviewing and intelligent debate about his books, and for the first time may be able to derive profit from criticism, because the critics know what they are talking about.

Inevitably such a climate of opinion encouraged a new breed of children's publishers and editors. When the first edition of this book was written there were less than a dozen publishers who maintained editorial departments specially for children's books, and not more than five or six specialist children's editors. In 1970 there are some sixty publishers actively engaged in children's books and The Children's Book Circle, an informal group of men and women working in the children's book departments of publishing firms, has ninety members.

Other developments emphasised the improved status of children's books in Britain. In 1966, after a one-day conference at the Holborn Library, a Joint Committee for Children's Books was formed. Three years later, in 1969, this was enlarged to create a more formal committee to be known by the impressive-sounding title of The Joint Consultative Committee on Children's Books (how far away the Sunday School reward days seem!). Membership consisted of two representatives each from the Library Association, the Booksellers' Association, the Publishers' Association, the National Book League, the Society of Authors and the School Library Association, with a single representative from the British Museum. What, if anything, the Committee actually accomplishes is not known, but that so many important bodies, between them representing all the interests involved in children's books (except children and parents!) should have come together is indicative of the new importance of writing for children.

This was also emphasised by the remarkable success of a conference held, in August 1969, at St Luke's College, Exeter, on 'Recent Children's Fiction and its Role in Education'. No less than two hundred and twenty people attended, including teachers, lecturers from colleges of education and university departments of education, and writers. A second conference followed in August 1970 which was notable for some lively discussion between authors and audience, and for a provocative piece of special pleading by Peter Dickinson, 'In Defence of Rubbish'. Most of the papers given at these conferences, and some of the discussions, are reprinted in a new journal, *Children's Literature in Education*.

Two recent developments, one parent-slanted, the other strictly professional, have been the bringing together on a national basis of the many local groups of parents originally established by Anne Wood under the title of 'Books for Your Children' groups, and the strong promotion by John Rowe Townsend and others of a National Centre for Children's Literature. The impressively-named Federation of Children's Book Groups is something that can only be admired. From a distance it seems to bear some resemblance to the parent-orientated Children's Book Councils in Australia, with which I am nowadays more familiar. Some of the activities of these Councils are inclined to make a professional's hair stand on end, but over the years I have learned to appreciate their true value and admire the work they do in making better books known to parents and children. A National Centre for Children's Literature seems less immediately necessary, but if it does no more than establish a national reference collection of children's books—the need for which was mentioned twenty years ago in the first edition of this book—it will serve a useful purpose. And as yet another sign of the increasing public awareness of the importance of children's books it can only be welcomed.

Finally, just as the final draft of this book was being completed, yet another new periodical was announced. This is *Signal*, edited by Nancy Chambers, the former editor, as Nancy Lockwood, of *Children's Book News*, and its aim is to provide a platform for writers 'whose ideas about and interests in children's books cannot be contained in brief reviews and articles'. Every party to the debate about children's books therefore now has a voice—except one. All that remains is for some interested person to launch yet another journal, devoted this time to the views of the children themselves about children's books, and the circle will be complete.

It was only to be expected that such a dramatic change in public opinion towards children's books should produce a corresponding change in the policies of publishers. Once a few publishers had been able successfully to demonstrate that it was possible to sustain a list from books of the highest quality only—and to make money from them—others soon followed. By the middle 'sixties the better-class children's book, the type of book that became known as a 'librarian's book', had become a standard to which the shrewd and successful could repair. There were, naturally enough, insufficient authors of real stature to supply all publishers with books, but the formula could be followed and the distinctive production style that a few publishers had evolved for this new type of children's fiction could be fairly easily copied. It was interesting to see publishers who had for so long regarded with disdain the methods and styles of others now following them in production style, editorial treatment and even the tone of their advertising.

The book to succeed became the 'better book for children'; to succeed it must carry on its face and on its pages the recognisable stamp of such a book, so as to be identifiable by the right kind of parent or librarian; and so publisher after publisher followed the pattern. Inevitably, imitation dilutes the overall level of quality and that has to some extent now occurred with children's books. But the improved quality of reviewing has compensated for this (though even in this field success is beginning to produce imitators) and the general level of new children's books is now astonishingly high.

What this new type of late-twentieth-century British children's book was concerned with will be examined in detail later. Some general developments should, however, be noted. No one looking for the first time at the books of the past twenty years could fail to notice the curious contradiction between two parallel trends. On the one hand we find critics, librarians, teachers, writers, preaching the need for an ever-increasing social realism—and authors doing their best to meet this need. On the other, an extraordinary revival and re-creation of folk-tales, fairy stories, fantasies, allegories, myths and legends which combine to produce an escape from reality, or a turning to a simpler kind of truth, so massive that it must surely indicate a profound need by present-day children.

One of the most remarkable developments of this has been the curious cult of pseudo-myth. Probably Professor Tolkien can claim credit for beginning this, with his first adventure of the Hobbits, published in 1937. But C. S. Lewis followed soon after the war with the first of the 'Narnia' books, *The Lion, The Witch and the Wardrobe*. Tolkien's *The Lord of the Rings* published a few years later, though apparently not written for children, was very soon claimed by them and seems to have established a vogue that has been followed by many other writers. Most of them would disclaim imitation, but the influence of these two great originals can clearly be seen in many subsequent books of this curious kind by various authors.

What this kind is, is worth analysis. It is a sort of saga, which can be read as an adventure story and is exciting enough to carry the reader along, if he wishes, with no thought of meaning or purpose; but which nevertheless, though seemingly a fantasy, is about real people and real issues, and with a strong moral flavour. The issues between right and wrong are clearly defined (it is so much easier to do this between Gandalf and Saruman, or Aslan and The White Witch than it is between a well-meaning parent and a difficult child, or a misguided delinquent and the law) and when right wins it does so directly and simply, with no agonising doubts or qualifications. A little reflection along these lines can tell us much that is revealing about today's children.

As does the equally remarkable revival of interest in poetry. Twenty years ago a publisher who took poetry for children seriously was asking for trouble. Despite, or perhaps to some extent because of the success of *Now We Are Six*, verse for children was disliked by parents and children alike. No one wanted to publish it and if any publisher was rash enough to do so, no one bought it. Nowadays poetry for children is a publishing success. And not only poetry written for children, but also special editions of such poets as Edward Thomas, Edmund Blunden, Emily Dickinson and many others who may be thought accessible to young readers. There are special series of poets for children, collected volumes of children's verse, and innumerable anthologies. As with the newer picture books it is now difficult to recognise when and how this began, but it seems possible that a precursor was a fine collection of poems for children, *Thomas and the Sparrow* by Ian Serraillier, which perhaps caught the public eye because of its brilliant scraperboard black and white illustrations by the Belgian artist, Mark Severin.

Parallel with these two developments has been a dramatic improvement in the quality of historical fiction for children—in itself another form of escape, though the better books are far more than that, having a reality of their own kind. Writers such as Rosemary Sutcliff, Ronald Welch and Stephanie Plowman have raised this type of fiction to a level at which it almost ceases to become writing for children and becomes simply fiction of the highest quality, readable at any level. This has also occurred with the best writers of modern fantasies. If one had to name half a dozen books only from the past twenty years, two at least on my list would be of this kind, *Tom's Midnight Garden* and *The Children of Green Knowe*.

The current strengthening of interest in witches, especially in books for girls, may well be part of the same development. Children have always been fascinated by witches, but until recently few authors thought of them as a likely subject for children's stories. There are now so many books about witches, or with witchcraft as the main or an associated theme, that a London library even produced a printed list of them. With these books also, although the idea seems at first exotic (and that is doubtless part of the fascination), it seems probable that their real attraction lies in the same sort of simplicity that draws children to the pseudo-myth. Like the goodies and the baddies in the western films, with their black hats and white hats, the reader is never in any doubt between right and wrong. A witch is obviously a bad thing. Occasionally a writer with a sense of humour rings the changes on this idea and presents us with a goodish sort of witch, as did John Onslow with his Stumpfs, but in the main these books consist of a simple conflict between a bad witch and a boy or girl representing the forces for good.

Evidence seems to be accumulating that our present-day children are in need of reassurance; that they are made uneasy by alarmingly true stories of unhappy lives, with their so often unresolved conflicts and the disturbing challenges to conventional ideas of right and wrong that they present; and that, as a natural and logical escape from this too-early emphasis on the unresolvable conflicts which instinct warns them they will have to face later in life, they turn to fairy tales and folk-lore, to myths, legends and fantasies—and to poetry.

As mentioned earlier, one of the most remarkable developments in publishing for children during the past twenty years has been the great number of editions of folk-tales, myths, legends, fairy tales and all those kinds of stories, however they may be defined, which as Elizabeth Cook put it:

> . . . are not realistic; they are almost unlocalized in time and space; they are often supernatural or at least fantastic in character; and the human beings in them are not three-dimensional people with complex motives and temperaments. These stories do hold a mirror up to nature, but they do not reflect the world as we perceive it with our senses at the present moment.[1]

[1] Elizabeth Cook, *The Ordinary and the Fabulous*, Cambridge University Press, 1969.

Illustration by Brian Wildsmith for *Mother Goose*
(Oxford University Press).

Illustration by Charles Keeping from his book *Through the Window*
(Oxford University Press).

There have been so many different editions of these stories that it would be impracticable even to list them here. Some of them have been conscientious, carefully researched attempts to breathe genuinely new life into old tales. Others have represented no more than publishing expediency (folk tales are selling, so we must have more folk tales). But this is not the place for an examination of that issue. This book is concerned with original creative writing and however grateful we may be to the devoted workers in the field for the pleasure they have given to children, editions of folk tales are seldom original and can hardly qualify as creative. For anyone who is genuinely interested in this topic I cannot recommend too highly Elizabeth Cook's *The Ordinary and the Fabulous*, an examination of the stories themselves, their sources, and their place in children's reading and thinking that is one of the most informative—and best written—books on children's literature to appear for many years.

Whether or not children have turned to such stories for escape from reality, whatever they turn to publishers will very quickly give it to them and it is interesting to observe the different policies of publishers in the paperback series which have been an important development in the latter part of the 'sixties. For many years the pioneer and still the best series, Puffin, was alone in the field. There were sound reasons for this. The basic conception of a paperback series is that it should bring together only the very *best* and best selling of a particular kind of book—because only by so doing can a publisher ensure that a large enough quantity of each title will be sold. 'Best selling' unhappily is not always synonymous with 'best' but with Puffins it was and no titles were included solely because they had sold well. Every book included represented a value judgement by the editor, and that was the great strength of the series. Few publishers had sufficient best-selling titles on their lists to build a paperback series of this kind. It made better sense, therefore, to permit those of their books which had the potential for a sale in paperbacks to be republished in the Puffin series, which thus included a selection of the best of British children's books of the period. A few publishers were reluctant to permit their books to appear as Puffins, and some authors preferred to limit their sales to hard-bound books at their original prices. But by 1960 the majority of the best children's authors had some at least of their books in Puffins, which thus became a reliable guide for parents to the good British children's books

—surely the real justification for such a series. Any cheap paperback series makes books more readily accessible to children, but a series without standards makes too much in-different work too readily accessible. It was the wide-ranging selectivity of the early Puffin list that made it so important, and so valuable—and so completely different from the majority of later paperback series, which all too often included little more than publishers' merchandise.

Throughout the 'fifties and 'sixties the adult paperback became an ever-strengthening cult. To many readers there seemed to be a kind of mystique about paperbacks, making them something essentially different and more appealing than books bound in hard covers. Everyone, therefore, wanted to 'get into paperbacks' and the result was a proliferation of series competing savagely for the limited number of authors whose books were capable of sustaining the sales of 50,000 or 100,000 copies that a paperback must achieve if it is to be profitable.

It was not long before the same motives led other pub-lishers of children's books into the paperback field. The first new series after Puffins was Armada Books. This was soon seen to be a bringing together of the tried and tested rather than the best, such authors as Enid Blyton, W. E. Johns and Richmal Crompton predominating. Other series followed. Dragon Books contained more of the same, with a further reduction in standard brought about by abridgement; the Story-Hour Library introduced 'processed' classics; but it soon became apparent that most publishers saw paperbacks for children as little more than a new kind of 'reward'. Most series contain a few better books—Monica Edwards in the Armada books, for example—but, in general, discriminating parents should look hard before buying cheap paperbacks for children. Classics have been not only abridged but bowdlerized as well and it is advisable before buying to read a few pages of a book you know, to test it for 'revision' and also to check its length. Most sensible parents would agree that it is better to do without *David Copperfield* than to read it in a 150-page version, which may also have been 'improved'.

Some of the latest paperback series, however, are on dif-ferent lines. Knight Books, Jets and Zebras contain newer and on the whole better work, more suited to the needs of the basically non-reading public at whom most children's paper-backs appeared to be aimed, and Topliners are an interesting development (see p. 150). Some publishers of children's books

with distinguished lists have also evolved paperback formats
in which to reprint a selection of their own better-selling
books (but without, apparently, having felt the need for
catching series titles). These are, however, somewhat different from the general paperback trend.

The age at which children read particular kinds of books
has continued to contract during the past twenty years and in
the last decade publishers and writers have been taking a good
hard look at teenage reading. One approach to this problem
has been a deliberate seeking after realism, and the effects of
the permissive society are beginning to find their way into
this sort of book for children. A more interesting, and more
genuine development has been the introduction of what
appears to be the beginning of an altogether new kind of
writing for children. One publisher has described these books
as 'novels for new adults', others call them 'novels for older
children' and there are several variations on these themes.
Some of these books are little more than a normal children's
book with a love interest added, but the best of them have
enlarged the range of children's literature by creating a kind
of book which although no longer in any sense a 'children's
book' by any earlier definition of that phrase is nevertheless
not written for adults and is in some undefinable way recog-
nizably different from a book written for adults. But it is
already obvious, from their reception by critics, that books of
this kind are read and enjoyed by adults, and it may well come
about that such books will form a new category that can be
read with equal enjoyment by both children and adults.

The most obvious examples of this trend, and the ones most
often quoted are Alan Garner's *The Owl Service* and Leon
Garfield's *Smith*, but equally interesting of their own different
kinds are Stephanie Plowman's two historical novels about
the last days of Czarist Russia, *Three Lives for the Czar* and
My Kingdom for a Grave, and K. M. Peyton's *Flambards*.
K. M. Peyton's books are closest to the earlier kind of children's books and Stephanie Plowman's probably the furthest
removed, but none of these books would have been publish-
able as children's books twenty years ago. They are simply
novels and there seems little doubt that, although children
may not appreciate all of them immediately, books of this
kind fill a real need and there will be many more of them in
future.

Nevertheless, although there has been a number of interesting developments in the past twenty years, and a few fine books have been published, some aspects of the flood of paperbacks and books in series are all too reminiscent of earlier publishing trends in children's books and demonstrate that they will remain a profitable, if competitive, field for the enterprising publisher and are always likely to be greatly influenced by commercial considerations. Although, therefore, the British children's book has improved out of all recognition in the last twenty years it remains as much a matter for surprise as congratulation that so high a proportion of the best children's books of the century should have been first published in Britain.

They emerged, not as part of any consciously planned publishing programme, nor from any preconceived idea of what constitutes a good children's book, but seemingly almost by chance from a mass of indifferent publishing. Some of them set a fashion in their time, but in general they are solitary stars and best considered as individual books in their proper section, rather than as part of this historical survey. The dates of some significant ones are, however, given below as some indication of the strength of the British contribution to this century's children's books.

A FEW DATES

1898	*The Story of Little Black Sambo*	Helen Bannerman
1901	*The Tale of Peter Rabbit*	Beatrix Potter
	Five Children—and It	E. Nesbit
1903	*Johnny Crow's Garden*	Leslie Brooke
1906	*Peter Pan in Kensington Gardens*	J. M. Barrie
	Puck of Pook's Hill	Rudyard Kipling
1908	*The Wind in the Willows*	Kenneth Grahame
1912	*Peacock Pie*	Walter de la Mare
1924	*When We Were Very Young*	A. A. Milne
1931	*Swallows and Amazons*	Arthur Ransome
1937	*Little Tim and the Brave Sea Captain*	Edward Ardizzone
	Orlando—the Marmalade Cat	Kathleen Hale
	The Hobbit	J. R. R. Tolkien

1938	*The Sword in the Stone*	T. H. White
1945	*Captain Slaughterboard Drops Anchor*	Mervyn Peake
1947	*Collected Stories for Children*	Walter de la Mare
1950	*The Lion, the Witch, and the Wardrobe*	C. S. Lewis
1952	*The Borrowers*	Mary Norton
1954	*The Children of Green Knowe*	L. M. Boston
1955	*A Swarm in May*	William Mayne
	The Fellowship of the Ring	J. R. R. Tolkien
1958	*Tom's Midnight Garden*	Philippa Pearce
1962	*ABC*	Brian Wildsmith

II. Books with Pictures

At the beginning of the century British children's picture books were dominated by three great artists whose work had achieved an international reputation. Books by Walter Crane, Randolph Caldecott, and Kate Greenaway continued to sell in large numbers throughout the first fifty years of the century, but there is nothing of the twentieth century about them. Even in their own day Caldecott and Kate Greenaway were already looking backward and setting their scenes in an earlier and in many ways largely mythical age. If the first half of this century had produced anything of equal stature to rival them they might perhaps by now have been superseded, but the level of picture books produced was on the whole such that until recently they were able to hold their own.

Nevertheless, although the general level has been low, there have been some brilliant exceptions, and one in particular to whom the whole world of children must be eternally indebted. Changing centuries are unlikely to diminish the ageless appeal of the books of Beatrix Potter, whose matchless style and meticulous, miniature water-colours combine to produce the most perfect series of stories ever designed for the entranced delight of children and their parents. Her first book, *The Tale of Peter Rabbit*, appeared in 1902. It was immediately successful and was followed at regular intervals by nineteen other little illustrated stories of the same kind (usually two a year). She also wrote and illustrated two others in the series, *The Tailor of Gloucester* and *The Tale of*

Little Pig Robinson, for slightly older children, and illustrated two books of nursery rhymes.

It is impossible to define the charm of a book by Beatrix Potter. The shape, the size, the colours used, the phraseology of the text, are all exactly right; but none of these physical qualities can explain why they go straight to the heart of every child who is lucky enough to have them read to him at the right age, and of every adult who does the reading. That secret, if it can be defined, must lie in the author's own loving-hearted delight in detail and the seriousness and complete absorption with which the stories are told. Children recognize immediately the absence of any suspicion of 'writing down' or even 'writing for children'. These are just stories which have miraculously come into being at one bound, complete and whole, for their delight, and children all over the world have in consequence accepted them as their own.

Drawing by L. Leslie Brooke for his book Johnny Crow's Garden (*Warne*).

Almost as good, in her own way, as Beatrix Potter, but less prolific and less able to sustain her output (and infinitely less of an artist) is Helen Bannerman, whose *The Story of Little Black Sambo* was published a few years before *The Tale of Peter Rabbit*. Helen Bannerman's gift for robust story-telling is unique and the unusual ingredients of her plots and the gaiety of her drawings make *Little Black Sambo* a riotous frolic that has entertained children and parents for fifty years and shows no sign of losing its popularity. Her other books are not quite so good. Children who love reading will always take *Little Black Quasha* to their hearts, for the idea of the tigers waiting until the book was finished has that inspired 'rightness' that children immediately recognize. But admirers of Helen Bannerman's work must regret the publication, in 1902, of a previously unpublished work, *Little Black Quibba*, which was repetitive of earlier work and added nothing to her reputation.

Beatrix Potter and Helen Bannerman were both always author-illustrators and both worked mostly in colour. Leslie Brooke, whose work became popular about the same time, did his best work in line, and much of it was as an illustrator of nursery rhymes and tales, rather in the Walter Crane tradition, although the verses which link the illustrations in his most famous books, *Johnny Crow's Garden*, *Johnny Crow's Party*, and *Johnny Crow's New Garden*, were his own.

Brooke achieved a reputation in the United States almost equal to that of his predecessors, but his work never became quite so well known in his own country. Although his colour is inclined to be monotonous and unimaginative his line drawings are full of vigour and packed with that concentrated understanding and sympathetic observation of background detail that children enjoy so much. He had an unrivalled gift for depicting action, and there is a sense of animation about his drawings which is lacking in much contemporary work. His animals are carefully and realistically drawn and he had a gift of making it appear that the odd antics which he makes them perform are perfectly natural. His quaint verses have an odd charm and his drawings a sense of fun, so that it is not surprising that young children should still enjoy the antics of cocksure and confident Johnny Crow.

Beatrix Potter, Helen Bannerman, and Leslie Brooke all produced their best work at the beginning of the century and there was for nearly a score of years thereafter hardly anything of enduring value produced in this field. The best illustrators of the day were drawn into a curiously sterile and uncreative by-way now almost forgotten, the 'fine art' or 'gift' book, and little creative work was done. The gift book originated with the lavish edition of *Peter Pan in Kensington Gardens* produced in 1906 with illustrations by Arthur Rackham, and for many years thereafter no publishing season was complete without half a dozen of these exotic extravagances, until as a result of over-production the public became sated and the publishers exhausted their own market. The two best known artists of the time were Arthur Rackham and Edmund Dulac. Their work was widely admired and many of the large number of volumes they produced became collector's pieces, but they were in their original form too sumptuous and expensive to be considered as genuine children's books. Many of the Rackham illustrations achieved a wider currency in later years in cheaper editions but their vogue soon passed. Other promising artists were drawn into work of this kind and few seem to have thought of devoting their time to the creation of original picture books. The series of picture-story books by Margaret and Mary Baker, decorated with charming silhouettes in black and white, was a pleasant novelty, reflecting a passing interest in scissor cuts and lightning silhouettes; and a rare gleam of light among the many nondescript 'animal picture books' and imitation Beatrix Potters that were almost the only alternative to the gift books in the bookshops of the time was William Nicholson's *Clever Bill*, published in 1928. This was followed the year after by his better known *The Pirate Twins*, a gay, witty and imaginative effort that was one of the first successful British children's books to be printed in colour by lithography on a matt surface paper.

Illustration by Mary Baker for Polly Who Did As She Was Told, *by Margaret Baker* (*Blackwell*).

The real twentieth-century picture book began to emerge in the nineteen-thirties. The first impulse undoubtedly came from the United States, where a group of cosmopolitan artists had begun to produce large and exciting books with a new approach to the use of colour in children's books, splashing it broadly and generously on the page and discarding the conventional 'pretty-pretty' approach which had for the past twenty years vitiated most of the British picture books. The books they produced gave children for the first time a chance of experiencing for themselves the impact of contemporary feeling in art, but there was much initial opposition to them in this country.

These new picture books also aimed at something more than had been attempted in the past. Many were instructive as well as entertaining, and although the conception was so easy to copy that the pattern soon became debased, the best of the early examples were a brilliant contribution to the development of children's books.

The distinguishing feature of all these new American picture books was the use of colour lithography, by which full-colour illustrations could be printed on cartridge and other rough-surfaced papers, in place of the traditional colour half-tone, which has to be specially printed on 'art' paper with its glossy surface. The way in which the text and illustrations are put down together on the printing plate in the lithographic process also makes it possible for the artist to design his book as a much more homogeneous whole than is possible with the rigid separation between text and illustrations necessitated by the use of line or half-tone blocks. This complete fusion of text and illustration is a characteristic feature of the twentieth-century picture book.

Other influences also were at work. Successful French children's books, notably the admirable Père Castor books and the inimitable Babar had found their way into British homes, though not initially in large numbers, and it was probably from France that the auto-lithographic technique, which has distinguished the best British picture books from their American rivals, originated.

It is not easy to remember how it all started. So many people seem to have had the same idea at about the same time that it is difficult to decide who first started the practice of the artist doing his original drawings direct on to the printer's plate. There were many difficulties to be overcome and the co-operation of fine printers in this research is a feature of the period. It is perhaps invidious to mention names, but the firms of Lund Humphries and W. S. Cowell were especially prominent, and the latter deserve a special mention not only for their association with three of the most distinctive picture books of the day—the original Babar, and his British successors, Orlando and Little Tim—but also with the development of Puffin Picture Books.

The two most successful British picture book series of this period produced by lithography were Kathleen Hale's exuberantly colourful chronicles of the adventures of *Orlando— the Marmalade Cat*, and Edward Ardizzone's more restrained but in some ways more endearing series of stories about Little Tim, of which the first was *Little Tim and the Brave Sea Captain*, one of the most convincing British picture story books yet produced. The Ardizzone books were almost the only modern British picture books to be as successful in the United States as in this country. They were, indeed, initially more successful in America, for Ardizzone's slightly sophisticated use of colour was often disliked by conventional parents in this country, many of whom denied themselves the pleasure of watching the delighted enjoyment with which children, whose sense of colour and design is uninhibited, absorb them.

No other author-illustrators of the immediately post-war period were able to equal the sustained success of Ardizzone and Kathleen Hale, but there were several distinguished single books, and at least one important series worthy of mention. Probably the best of the single books were Stephen Bone's and Mary Adshead's *The Little Boy and his House* and *The Little Boys and their Boats*, the only completely successful British examples of 'picture-stories with a purpose'. Other artists who produced colourful picture books were Jack Townend, Leslie Wood, and Hilary Stebbing. Townend's *A Railway ABC* and *A Story About Ducks* should confound anyone who attempts to argue that children dislike modern drawings, while Leslie Wood's illustrations for Diana Ross's books about her *Little Red Engine* have a gay insouciance that delights children. A later book, also by Diana Ross, *Whoo, Whoo, the Wind Blew*, was less successful, probably because conventional parents objected to the joyous abandon with which the artist depicted corsets and lingerie floating through the air in an amusing double spread of colour (how remote such a reaction seems today!). Hilary Stebbing wrote and illustrated one of the most amusing war-time picture books, *Maggie the Streamlined Taxi,* and also produced two other starkly colourful stories, *Monty's New Car* and *Freddie and Ernest.*

Joan Kiddell-Monroe's *In his Little Black Waistcoat,* one of the first books to use as a model the appealing panda, was remarkable for its fearless use of white space, at a time when most conventional picture books appeared to be designed upon the principle of giving the public as many colours as possible and as much drawing as the page would hold. Another artist who specialised in animals was Clifford Webb, whose *The Story of Noah* was an attractive and colourful retelling in a pleasantly secular manner. Other books of his were *Butterwick Farm, Jungle Picnic,* and *The North Pole Before Lunch.* His use of colour was more restrained than that of most artists of the day and, although his books were reproduced by lithography, they often looked more like woodcuts, which probably accounted for his popularity even with those sections of the public that did not normally like 'modern' children's books.

A more controversial artist was Mervyn Peake, whose *Captain Slaughterboard Drops Anchor* became a focus of argument for those who strongly resented the encroachment of contemporary illustrative techniques into children's books. Printed on blue, pink, and yellow paper, with grotesque and even macabre-looking figures scattered in seeming incoherence about its pages, it had the most unusual appearance of any British picture book of its time and it is not altogether surprising that so many people should have been startled by it. Even today, accustomed as we now are to the extravagant colourfulness of artists like Wildsmith, Burningham or Keeping, Peake's vivid grotesques stand out starkly, with a quality that is all their own. But children are commonly a good deal tougher than parents appear to imagine, and most of them seem to enjoy the fantastic creatures of Peake's imagination. These, if considered as line drawings apart from their background of garish colour, are really very little different from the grotesque animals and figures that were popular in children's books at the end of the last century. Peake may or may not have been a 'children's artist' but he was one of the most original draughtsmen to work with children's books in this century and his illustrations have often a quality of inspired interpretation. His set of drawings for Grimm's *Household Tales,* for example, is the finest since Cruikshank.

Drawing by Mervyn Peake for Household Tales, *by the Brothers Grimm (Eyre and Spottiswoode).*

The most significant development before 1950, however, was neither in picture books proper, nor in picture story books, but in the adaptation of modern illustrative and printing techniques to the production of an entirely new kind of informative picture book. Sometimes these books have a story, usually rather a feeble one, but the best of them are unashamedly and forthrightly instructional. The subjects dealt with are often of a far more complicated kind than can be readily assimilated by a child of the age that normally reads books looking like picture books, and this fact caused some initial misunderstandings about their purpose; but the genre is now well established and the success of some brilliant examples soon influenced the appearance and technique of many types of more definitely educational books. Now, in the late 'sixties and early 'seventies, such techniques are taken for granted and it is difficult to remember when informative books, whether for children or adults, were produced in any other way. The combination of illustration and text has become so complete that in the best examples they are inseparable. It comes as a surprise, therefore, to be reminded how comparatively recent this development really is.

The first books of this kind were the Puffin Picture Books, which came into being through the collaboration of a creative and original-minded designer and editor, a courageous publisher, and an enterprising and experimentally-minded printer. Noel Carrington, who designed the first Puffin Picture Books, started thinking on these lines after examining a series of cheaply produced Russian picture books which were then selling at the equivalent of a penny. His idea was to combine the auto-lithographic plate directly hand-drawn by the artist (thus saving photographic and retouching charges) and the modern fast-running lithographic printing press, with the object of producing inexpensive picture books which would bring the work of the best contemporary artists within the reach of the smallest purse. The result was the Puffin Picture Books, a series of sixteen-page paper-covered books of a then unusual oblong shape which set a completely new style in picture books. The formula was easy enough to copy, once someone had worked it out, and there were soon so many imitators of their superficial features that a positive reaction against these 'flats' (as they came to be called in the bookshops) set in and virtually drove them out of existence. The best Puffin Picture Books are, however, still unchallenged and they made a most distinctive contribution to contemporary picture books.

Their characteristic feature (apart from the purely physical aspect) was a carefully thought-out use of illustration, combined with a simplified text, to communicate the basic facts about all manner of subjects that are capable of being assimilated visually. The best examples succeed admirably, and it is regrettable that the series appears to have been a casualty of post-war publishing economics. Although a few of the more popular titles still survive, the majority are out of print and the series appears to be moribund, the name Puffin now being more readily associated in the public mind with the Puffin Story Books. (The contemporary Picture Puffins are completely different, being a picture book equivalent of the story Puffins, consisting as they mainly do of reprints of other publishers' picture books.)

The same technique has since been used with larger and more expensive books. The first of these was Clark Hutton's *A Picture History of Britain*, a successful attempt to make history interesting to quite young readers by vivid illustrations which occupy more space than the text. Two other interesting examples were *The Map That Came to Life* and *Houses*. *The Map That Came to Life* by H. J. Deverson and Ronald Lampitt, is an imaginative attempt to explain the conventional map symbols by means of a series of colourful illustrations, each of which interprets a section of an imaginary ordnance map. The illustrations are linked together by a rather youthful story; this tends to limit the appeal of the book, which would probably have been better as pure instruction. A later book by the same author, *The Open Road*, deals with road signs and the plotting in the same way of a journey by car instead of foot. *Houses*, by Margaret and Alexander Potter, which was in many ways better, went to the other extreme and combined a set of brilliantly interpretative drawings with an extremely adult and in some parts complex text which made no concessions at all. This book, which traced the development of house construction in Britain throughout the centuries, was one of an admirable series, *The Changing Shape of Things*, all the titles in which, although none of the others were as suavely accomplished or attractive to look at as *Houses*, made use of the same technique of instructing visually by arousing interest. The books are difficult to classify, because they are neither purely educational nor intended purely for pleasure reading; they are, moreover, neither written obviously for children nor for adults. An intelligent child of twelve should be able to enjoy them, while a dull-witted adult probably would not. They are in fact an excellent example of a new kind of children's book which is one of the twentieth century's distinctive contributions—a book which attempts, by combining educational and leisure reading and setting no apparent age level, to enlarge its scope by appealing to all markets.

There are now so many fine examples that it is difficult to select without doing injustice to those omitted. Representative of different aspects of the genre, however, are C. Walter Hodges' series, *The Story of Britain*, which includes *The Spanish Armada*, *Magna Carta* and *The Norman Conquest*; Alan Sorrell's *Saxon England*, *Roman England*, *Norman England* and, a later book, *Nubia: A Drowning Land*; Papas's brilliantly incisive commentaries on *The Press*, *Parliament*,

The Law and *The Church*; Helen and Richard Leacroft's *The Buildings of Ancient Egypt* (and *Greece* and *Rome*); Victor Ambrus's *The Merchant Navy*, *The Royal Navy*, *The Royal Air Force* and *The British Army*; and two compelling books by Ian Ribbons, *Monday 21 October 1805* and *Tuesday 4 August 1914*. In slightly different vein are Edward Osmond's *A Valley Grows Up* and *The Thames Flows Down*, and Pauline Baynes's illustrations and decorations for *A Dictionary of Chivalry*, which transform what could have been only a reference book into a rare delight—and won her the 1968 Kate Greenaway medal.

In the years immediately following the war the early objections to the work of such artists as Ardizzone and Kathleen Hale began slowly to disappear. Younger parents, with a new generation of children brought up in a different atmosphere—and at a time when many of the older books were temporarily unobtainable—were readier to accept unconventional-looking books. There was less prejudice in the air generally and it began to be seen that illustrations of this kind were more in keeping with the century in which we live. Just as, with music, the work of such composers as Prokofiev and Stravinsky ceased to be booed by audiences and came to seem positively tuneful (to those with ears to hear) so the work of early picture book innovators came to seem almost conventional. Influential folk like the buyers in bookshops and libraries, and even the publishers' production managers and sales staffs, were themselves younger and more open-minded.

Such a change in climate soon produces new flowers and it was not long before artists appeared to take advantage of this new freedom. As with so many developments in children's books, it is not easy to put a date to the beginning of this new step forward. The general standard of illustration had been improving steadily. By 1961 the illustration of children's books had become one of the most important outlets for the work of artists of all kinds. In that year 2,500 new books for children's leisure reading were published, the majority of which were illustrated. A field that traditionally had seemed something of a Cinderella courted only by a specialist few, had suddenly become both important and rewarding, and one to be acknowledged by art schools as something for which training was worth while.

Illustration by Helen
Bannerman for her book
*The Story of Little Black
Quasha* (Chatto and Windus).

Illustration by Leslie Wood for
*The Story of the Little
Red Engine*, by Diana Ross
(Faber).

Illustration by Edward Ardizzone from his book *Little Tim and the Brave Sea Captain* (Oxford University Press).

Illustration by Raymond Briggs from *The Mother Goose Treasury* (Hamish Hamilton).

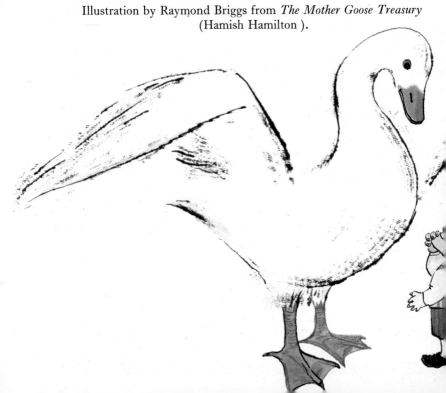

The combined pressures for better artists for children's books and for a new kind of artist for advertising work of special kinds brought about a reformation in the art schools. The book illustrator (which implied, of course, a children's book illustrator, for illustrated adult fiction had virtually disappeared) became a respected professional with a field of his own, instead of being regarded as simply a failed painter. And he was better trained, more capable of taking advantage of the newer techniques of reproduction and printing, because at last instruction in the practical business of drawing or painting for reproduction had been separated from the traditional 'art course', with its endless hours of figure drawing and excessive preoccupation with representational painting.

It was from this atmosphere of freedom from inhibitions, combined with an intense professionalism, that the children's book artists of the last decade arose; almost, it seemed, from a kind of spontaneous combustion. One minute, it now appears looking back, we were all reasonably satisfied with the sort of illustrations to which we had been accustomed for the past twenty years—and then there was Wildsmith. Other artists, no doubt, were at work at the same time; other books of roughly the same kind were published, or about to be published, but it was the early work of Brian Wildsmith that accomplished the first breakthrough, and for a time aroused much the same sort of antagonism as had the earlier modernists. He is a prolific artist, obviously working best at full stretch, when he has a lot of work in hand, and it must have taken a courageous publisher to commission so much work in colour, in so short a time, from a then relatively unknown artist. In the space of five years between 1961 and 1966 he illustrated an *ABC*, editions of a number of La Fontaine's fables; a collection of poems for children edited by Edward Blishen; *A Child's Garden of Verses*; *The Arabian Nights* and a *Mother Goose*, all in full colour—and what colour! Before the *ABC* he had illustrated a number of children's books in line, using colour only for the jackets, but his black and white work has never been so successful as his colour and it is as the leading exponent of the exuberantly colourful contemporary picture book that he is best known. He is still hard at work, having recently produced three enchanting volumes of *Birds*, *Wild Animals* and *Fishes* and a delightful *Circus*. There seems as yet no sign of his running out of steam. He is an artist to whom a whole generation of children must already be

D

grateful and whose work is likely to live a long time. The child who has never been fortunate to see, better still own, a Wildsmith (for he needs to be lived with) has missed an unforgettable experience.

An artist whom many critics link with Wildsmith is John Burningham, whose *Borka, the Adventures of a Goose with No Feathers* was a Kate Greenaway Medal winner in 1963. His colour is almost equally brilliant, but more controlled, more immediately accessible, and there are many who consider that his books appeal to more children than do Wildsmith's. He has illustrated many books, of many kinds. Like Wildsmith, he has done an *ABC*, but he has also done a number of beautiful books of his own, including *Trubloff, Cannonball Simp, Humbert, Mr. Firkin, and the Lord Mayor of London, Seasons, Harquin* and *Mr Gumpy's Outing* all lit by a controlled delight in colour and a strong sense of fun. He has also produced a number of large drawings in colour for use as wall friezes or decorations. *Birdland, Storyland, Lionland, Wonderland, Jungleland* are all eight-foot friezes which must have added new dimensions to many a nursery wall—and many teenagers' rooms also. His book, *Seasons*, also contains four large posters, $22\frac{1}{4}''$ by $17\frac{1}{2}''$, which are better on a wall than in the book. It is difficult to think of any twentieth-century artist, with the possible exceptions of Ardizzone and Ernest Shepard, who has given children more pleasure and there can surely be no other family in the world with *two* medal winners, for Burningham is married to Helen Oxenbury, whose illustrations for *The Quangle-Wangle's Hat* won the Kate Greenaway Medal in 1969.

Charles Keeping, on the other hand, seems less obviously interested in giving pleasure. His colour is almost as brilliant as Wildsmith's; he has a strangely hypnotic style which seems to be either greatly liked or strongly detested; and he is unusual among what are perhaps too loosely described as 'picture book artists' in being passionately interested in ideas. In a contribution on 'Illustration in Children's Books' to the first number of *Children's Literature in Education*, he had a number of things to say about his work which, although convincing and of great value to anyone trying to understand what such an artist is trying to achieve, make one wonder whether the age for which picture books are still, presumably, produced, is really a suitable one for the introduction of such conceptions. His work is extremely sophisticated; to get the full benefit from it the reader should really understand what the artist is seeking to communicate; but for what age, one wonders, is it intended?

Charles Keeping originally made his name as an illustrator in black and white. Some of his work in this field was greatly admired—a set of dramatic illustrations for one of Rosemary Sutcliff's books for example—but much of it aroused strong dislike from some children and critics. His work in line is stark, compelling, theatrically effective and whether it succeeds or fails, never negligible. He is, one feels, an artist first and an illustrator second, and nothing that he draws is carried out in the way any other artist would have treated the same theme. But despite the vividness of his line drawings he first came into real prominence with a series of books in full colour which he produced as both artist and author, *Shaun and the Cart Horse, Charley, Charlotte and the Golden Canary* and *Alfie and the Ferryboat*. Some of his work in these books was immediately attractive because, despite what a few critics said, children could see immediately what was intended and *Charley, Charlotte and the Golden Canary* is a delight from beginning to end. But the beginnings of the style that many readers have criticised was already apparent in these books and his two later books, *Joseph's Yard* and *Through the Window* apparently indicate the direction in which he wishes to go. He is an exciting artist, whose work it is impossible not to admire, even if one does not always *like* it, and his future work promises to be as important as that of any artist working in children's books today. But it is difficult to see how such an approach can be carried much further without taking picture books directly into the area of social commentary and the age at which picture books are of value is still, I believe, too young for such conceptions.

Another brilliant artist who has worked both in this picture book field and in black and white illustration is William Stobbs, whose Kate Greenaway Medal winner *Kashtanka* was an entrancing fusion of text and illustration (the story is by Chekhov) and an interesting bridge between the early work in lithography of the pre-war artists and the Wildsmith-Burningham-Keeping era. Later books include versions of *The Three Billy Goats Gruff, Daniel in the Lion's Den*, and other stories. His work is especially attractive to children because although it has nearly all the infectious gaiety of colour that is present in the later books it is also still recognisably representational. As is also the work of Gerald Rose, whose *Old Winkle and the Seagulls* was another Kate Greenaway Medal winner. Many other artists have produced attractive work in colour: Antony Maitland (*Mrs Cockle's Cat*), Helen Oxenbury (*The Dragon of an Ordinary Family*, *The Great Big Enormous Turnip*, and *The Quangle-Wangle's Hat*), Errol Le Cain (*The Cabbage Princess* and *King Arthur's Sword*), William Papas (*Freddy the Fell Engine*, *No Mules*, *The Story of Mr Nero*), Pat Hutchins, whose *Rosie's Walk* and *The Surprise Party* introduced a delightful note of gaiety, and Shirley Hughes. There are a great many picture books in colour now being published in Britain and it would need a separate book to deal with them all adequately. This brief list is intended as no more than a signpost to a few of the better examples.

This section would not be complete without a note on the contemporary illustration of fiction. This century has seen the virtual extinction of the classic full-page line or colour drawing used with such success in the early part of the century by H. M. and C. E. Brock, Hugh Thompson, H. J. Ford, Charles Robinson and others. It has been replaced by the more flexible use of illustration, either as chapter heads and tails or as small drawings cut into or round the text as an integral part of the

Drawing by Laurian Jones for Alice and Thomas and Jane, *by Enid Bagnold (Heinemann).*

book. The characteristic American technique of lithographing the whole book so that sensitive chalk or pencil drawings can be reproduced on the text paper has not yet become widely used, but line blocks or woodcuts dropped in are common, and considerable pains are taken to link text and illustration into a homogeneous whole.

An interesting development was the use of deliberately child-like drawings. In the early examples the idea arose because the author wanted to make certain that the illustrations were accurate and so preferred to do them himself, but having had insufficient training as an artist to produce sophisticated drawings had to resort to this child-like technique. Hugh Lofting's illustrations for his Dr Dolittle books, Arthur Ransome's for his *Swallows and Amazons* and other books, and Professor Tolkien's for *The Hobbit* are the best-known examples of this trend—one which some artists deplore because they believe that it leads to a lowering of standards, an acceptance in the readers of less-than-the-best in the way of illustration. Some of these child-like drawings, of course, such as Laurian Jones's for *Alice and Thomas and Jane* or Pamela Whitlock's for *The Far Distant Oxus* actually were drawn by children. But the attractions of the idea were obvious and it was widely copied. Much of the better contemporary illustration also gives the impression of having been drawn by a child, but in a subtler and infinitely more sophisticated manner that is based upon first-class draughtsmanship.

The first half of the century was notable for a general raising of the standard of illustration rather than for outstanding individual work (with the possible exception of Mervyn Peake). The illustrator whose work gave most pleasure during that time was Ernest H. Shepard, whose delightful line drawings for *The Wind in the Willows* and A. A. Milne's books are as inimitable as the work of Tenniel. It is lamentable that in many recent editions of his work the reproduction is so poor that much of their delicacy is lost.

Other artists of this time worthy of mention were Rex Whistler, who illustrated an elegant edition of Hans Andersen's *Fairy Tales and Legends*; John and Isobel Morton Sale; Rowland Hilder, Jack Matthew, Philip Gough, and a group of artists, Robert Gibbings, Joan Hassall, Gwen Raverat, Eric Fitch Dagliesh and C. F. Tunnicliffe, whose work has figured in a twentieth-century revival of the woodcut. Eve Garnett's illustrations, to her own *The Family from One End Street* and other books, should also be mentioned.

Illustration by Rex Whistler for Fairy Tales and Legends,
by Hans Andersen (The Bodley Head).

Many of the artists working in this time maintained their
reputations, some even increasing them, in the later part of
the century. Harold Jones, whose illustrations to *This Year:
Next Year* had aroused unusual interest earlier, after the war
produced a fine set of illustrations for Kathleen Lines's selection of nursery rhymes, *Lavender's Blue*. He also illustrated
versions of *Noah and the Ark*, *The Pied Piper of Hamelin*,
Once in Royal David's City and *Jack and the Beanstalk*.
C. Walter Hodges, who had before the war collaborated in
many fine books and achieved signal success with his own
Columbus Sails, a superb example of what can be achieved by
an author-artist of calibre, won the Kate Greenaway Medal
in 1964 with his *Shakespeare's Theatre* and illustrated many
distinguished books, including his own series, *The Story of
Britain*, mentioned earlier, and a later book, *The Overland
Launch*. Joan Kiddell-Monroe, another successful pre-war
artist, became one of the most distinguished post-war illustrators, especially notable for her distinctive illustrations for
Oxford's *Myths and Legends* series.

In the past twenty years a completely new school of book illustrators has come into prominence. Outstanding among black and white artists have been Edward Ardizzone, William Stobbs and Charles Keeping, whose dramatic characterisations and bold designs for historical novels in particular have produced some memorable fusions of text and picture; Victor Ambrus, whose attractively descriptive work in both line and colour has been successful, and Robin Jacques whose unusual work has something of the quality of Mervyn Peake but who is perhaps not as successful with children as he is with adults. Leonard Rosoman is a distinguished painter who has produced some fine line illustrations for children, and there are so many other artists of high standard that it is surprising that publishers should ever be content with inferior work. Some are better liked than others—opinions differ, for example, about the caricaturish work of Papas, which seems at times not to help the books it illustrates (though his own books seem better suited to it) and not all children like the work of such artists as Alan Howard and Eric Fraser. But

Illustration by Joan Kiddell-Monroe for Welsh Legends and Folk-Tales, *retold by Gwyn Jones (Oxford University Press).*

Illustration by Alan Howard for The Faber Storybook,
edited by Kathleen Lines (Faber).

Margery Gill, Richard Kennedy, Diana Stanley, Susan Einzig,
Dick Hart, Geraldine Spence, Peggy Fortnum, Raymond
Briggs, Annette MacArthur Onslow, Fritz Wegner, Hilary
Abrahams, Gareth Floyd, and Shirley Hughes have all
produced work of distinction, some of which is illustrated
on the pages of this book.

With so much talent to choose from it is not surprising that
the best children's books are now better illustrated and
designed than they have ever been, but it is surprising that so
much poor work should still persist, not only in the cheap
series but sometimes unexpectedly in the books of publishers
who might be expected to know better. It is now generally
recognised that a poor set of illustrations can seriously harm
a book, not only with book buyers but also by reducing its
chances of communication with young readers. Today's children know more about pictures than any previous generation,
and their standards are far higher than most people catering
for them give them credit for. Providing a good book with a
good artist—and the right artist for that book—is as important a part of the work of a children's book department as
editing or designing—or selling—the finished product. Some
publishers excel in this, and their books are immediately

recognisable for it. Others appear to pick their artists from a hat, with results that are sometimes successful but more often as distressing to the reader as they must be to the authors.

Although there is now a sizeable literature on the illustration of children's books, little of it is concerned with the practical problems that face the publisher in choosing an appropriate illustrator, or the artist himself in tackling the task of illustrating a children's book successfully in line. It has not yet even been clearly established what constitutes success. To answer such questions one can turn only to children's own opinions on the one hand and on the other to the working philosophies that some artists have set down for the record. 'Knowing how children like to identify themselves with the chief characters in their book, I attempt to make the pictures as real as possible,' says Edward Ardizzone. Again, 'given a fine-art training, illustration is not a case of coming from the lofty heights of art with a capital "A", but rather a problem of adjusting oneself to a new set of values and some tricky customers,' says Gerald Rose.[1]

The artists, it is immediately apparent, concern themselves primarily with what children want. Too often the critics, and the designers of children's books, concern themselves with something different. The task of an illustrator is not necessarily to communicate to the young reader a set of values. If that can be done at the same time, so much the better. But the first task is to *illustrate*, to bring the characters and incidents in the book a little more alive, to illumine and enlarge the text.

That other task, the introduction to colour, to imagination and a heightened sense of reality—and to all the intangibles beyond or beside reality—has to be accomplished long before illustration begins. Children, if the opinions attributed to them in the few studies that have been undertaken can be relied on, want different things from the pictures in their books at different ages. The time for Wildsmith, Keeping and artists of their kind is when the child is very young, when his mind is completely without prejudice, unformed, and wide open to impressions of all kind. This is the age at which likes and dislikes, and unconscious value judgements are formed. As he grows older he begins to want the illustrations in his books to look more like the things that he sees. He does not

[1] 'Children's Book Illustration in England', *Penrose Annual*, 1962.

Drawing by Fritz Wegner for The Dribblesome Teapots and Other Incredible Stories, *by Norman Hunter (The Bodley Head).*

mind the artist's picture of them being enlarged, or heightened, but he does want to know what they are. If things, or actions, are described in the text he wants the illustrations of those things or action to be right. And it seems likely that he prefers them to be clear and simple. As a twelve-year-old reported in a study in 1962, pictures should 'show what matters, and not contain a lot of bushes, other people, and heaps of rotten old things which are only confusing'.[1]

There are still some artists working on children's books in Britain today who do confuse their drawings with 'lots of bushes and other rotten old things'—sometimes to conceal the fact that they can't draw feet or hands, or horses' necks, or ellipses, or surmount some other technical difficulty; more often because they believe that this kind of embellishment 'adds artistic verisimilitude to an otherwise bald and unconvincing narrative'. But the majority of British contemporary line artists are now genuine illustrators and the best of them are producing work that adds immeasurably to children's enjoyment of the books they are reading.

[1] 'Children and their Books', Anders Hedvall and Bror Zachrisson, *Penrose Annual*, 1962.

III. The In-Between Books

The twentieth-century's principal contribution to children's literature has been in the invention of fantastic and improbable adventures for that enchanted time when children are first beginning to experience the delights of fitting together a story in the mind. Not only do the greatest writers of the period all belong to this group; there is also a whole flock of lesser but still satisfactory authors whose work achieves distinction. This field is in fact the only one in the whole range of children's reading about which it is possible to say with confidence that there is no reason at all why the most voracious of young readers should ever be given anything but the best—for there is so much good work available that not only need the inferior, meretricious or shoddy book never be offered to him, but he is unlikely even to be able to read *all* the good ones.

There are several reasons for this twentieth-century phenomenon. It may or may not be the century of the common man, but it is certainly the century of the child. Never before have parents, especially fathers, been so much aware of their children as human beings, and never before have they taken such delight in observing their growing interest in the lives of animals and of the people round them. The period when children are most interesting intellectually is when they are ceasing to be infants and just beginning to think and act for themselves. Before that they are enchanting, and it is pleasant to watch their reactions to the pictures and stories offered to them, but what they are able to absorb is not yet the kind of story an intelligent man would be likely to want to create. Later they cease to be children and begin to grow away from that intimate and awakening awareness which has such a special fascination for writers. It is hardly surprising, therefore, that nearly all the distinguished writers who have turned to writing a book or books for children should have produced books of fantasy.

The early part of the century will almost certainly be noted in future histories of this kind of literature for the work of four writers: Rudyard Kipling, J. M. Barrie, Kenneth Grahame, and A. A. Milne. It would, at first sight, seem difficult to find four more dissimilar writers; yet their books were all influenced by similar factors, and their combined influence on other writers of the period and on the development of writing for children generally has been in a uniform direction.

All four wrote for children from a love of children and a real understanding not only of their likes and dislikes but of their natures. None of them wrote exclusively for children (all were in fact successful in other fields) and thus none of them was ever driven to lower his own standards by the necessity to produce new books regularly. All were more interested in giving children pleasure than in teaching them anything. Kipling alone shows traces of didacticism—it is particularly noticeable in the *Just So Stories*—but it is a new kind of didacticism. Above all, all four were genuinely creative writers, working in this field from a sincere impulse, usually the desire to tell a story to a particular child or group of children, and with complete integrity.

Kipling's contribution is too well known to call for more than mention, but his genius as an originator has received less than its due. *The Jungle Books* were something completely new in their day and initiated an entirely new way of writing about animals, as well as presenting to a score of writers the conception which is exemplified in the name Tarzan. There are aspects of *The Jungle Books* that are disturbing to contemporary susceptibilities and adults reading them aloud may find it necessary to skip many passages—especially those about the Jungle Law—but the conception is timeless and most children seem able to enjoy the books without harm. Kipling is a difficult writer to discuss in a book that needs some division into sections by approximate ages, because he is beyond classification. His books cover all ages. Beginning from the first read-aloud days with the *Just So Stories* (what parent who has read these aloud can ever forget the 'great grey-green greasy Limpopo River'?) he has something for every stage of childhood. *Stalky & Co.* was the first nearly natural boy's school story. Like *The Jungle Books*, it has some disconcerting features, but it was a completely new thing in its day, especially in its use of humour derived from character, and deserves to survive. The *Just So Stories*, although perhaps not quite so original, used the fabulous technique in a new way and have inspired a host of imitators. *Puck of Pook's Hill* and *Rewards and Fairies* were the forerunners of a new approach to the teaching of history, or, it would be more accurate to say, to the communication of a sense of history. *Captains Courageous* is an excellent sea-story-cum-unsatis-factory boy grows up story, of a kind that set new standards for its type. Finally, *Kim* was such an original conception that even now its achievement is not wholly appreciated.

It is to be hoped that no child is so unlucky as never to have met Mowgli. It is certain that hardly any twentieth-century child can have failed to encounter *Peter Pan*. And yet, although Mowgli is certainly one of the immortals, I have my doubts about the survival of *Peter Pan* as a book, though not as a story. The story of *Peter Pan* has been told in so many forms that only a fraction of the children who read it do so in Barrie's own words, but the tale itself is such an inspired amalgam of a dozen familiar and loved ingredients that it survives all adaptation. It may perhaps be more likely to live as a traditional nursery story, told in innumerable versions, like *Cinderella* or *Little Red Riding Hood*, than as an individual piece of creative writing. Whatever its future its immediate past was an overwhelming triumph, and the cause of an immense revival of interest in fairy stories.

Equally unquestionable is the permanence, as an inspired and characteristically English contribution to children's litera-ture, of Kenneth Grahame's *The Wind in the Willows*. It is not an easy book to write about, and it was, indeed, dismissed in one of those 'classified booklists' that are so numerous on the other side of the Atlantic as 'an amusing animal-story about a water-rat and a mole'. That description is true enough, as far as it goes, but how pitifully short it falls, even leaving out the magnificent Toad! Kenneth Grahame had already demon-strated in *Dream Days* and *The Golden Age* an apprehension of childhood that is almost unique (only de la Mare in our own time comes near it), and in *The Wind in the Willows* this instinctive understanding combined with the author's love of his small son Alistair to produce one of the most endearing books ever written for children.

There are surprisingly few really great books for children, and it is only when one remembers how many of the immortals were originally conceived not for children but adults— *Gulliver's Travels, Robinson Crusoe, The Pilgrim's Progress, The Arabian Nights, Don Quixote*—that one realises the full extent of the twentieth-century's contribution to children's literature, for all its finest children's books were written *for* children; and one of the greatest of these is *The Wind in the Willows*.

Part of the secret of the success of *The Wind in the Willows* is that its appeal is ageless and so parents never tire of reading it aloud. Like all great books it is inexhaustible, and one is always coming across some fresh delight. Perhaps a new

Drawing by Ernest Shepard for The House at Pooh Corner, *by A. A. Milne (Methuen).*

touch of human frailty in Toad, who is a true product of the English comic imagination; perhaps a sudden renewed delight (in an exile) of the English scene so lovingly delineated; perhaps a surprised appreciation (in a yachtsman reading it for the first time since his own childhood) of how perfectly Grahame has summed up in a single magical sentence the eternal masculine enjoyment of 'messing about in boats'—at each fresh reading the parent's delight is increased instead of dulled.

A. A. Milne's books also owe much of their success to their readability. The curious adult passion for his four books which was one of the features of that supposedly sophisticated age, the nineteen-twenties, resulted for a time in prejudicing many people, especially intellectuals, against them. Now, forty years later, it is possible to look at them objectively and realise how good they are. The two books of verses *When We Were Very Young* and *Now We Are Six*, although marred for some ears by occasional lapses into sentimentality, are at their best very good indeed. In accurate observation and interpretation of young children's activities and interests, and the reproduction of them in memorable metre, they are second only to *A Child's Garden of Verses*, and though they fall short, as poetry, of Walter de la Mare's *Peacock Pie*, which had appeared twelve years earlier, they have probably given as much pleasure to a wider range of children.

Milne's best work for children is in the two volumes of stories, *Winnie-The-Pooh* and *The House At Pooh Corner*, about the lovable animals which he created from his own son's toys. Pooh, the Bear of Very Little Brain; the melancholy donkey Eeyore; the irrepressible Piglet; the irresponsible Tigger, and the legendary Heffalump are known and loved in innumerable homes, and there is a stage in every child's development when these two books are exactly right.

Another considerable writer whose books still make very good reading, although of a rather different kind, is E. Nesbit, whose first book was published in 1899, and who continued a steady output until 1925. She differs from the four writers first discussed, in that after becoming a professional writer for children she produced books at regular intervals, which is probably why she produced no single outstanding book. She had, however, a sure sense of character, a nice control of incident and a delightfully natural conversational style that have combined to make her stories enjoyable to several generations of children.

Drawing by Gordon Browne for The Story of the Treasure Seekers, *by E. Nesbit (Benn).*

E. Nesbit is unusual among children's writers in being equally at home in fantasy and realism. Her Bastable stories are still among the few good stories of family life, and high on any list of fantasies must come the series of stories of everyday magic which she began in *Five Children—and It* and continued in *The Phoenix and the Carpet* and *The Story of the Amulet.* E. Nesbit's work is of special interest today because she was one of the very few writers of fiction for children in the early part of the century to sustain a regular output. She was able to do so without ever permitting her own standards to fall disastrously low—or producing a really bad book— because she was a true professional, working always well within her limits, and because she genuinely understood and *liked* children. Even in this latter part of a century, which has seen more change in manners and modes than any other, her children still seem natural and lifelike and are accepted by contemporary readers because their characters are so clearly and honestly observed and their humour is genuinely child-like, not simply the superimposed adult humour so often substituted by inferior writers.

Later in time than Nesbit was Hugh Lofting, with his stories of Dr Dolittle, the man who could talk to animals. I feel a little uneasy about claiming Hugh Lofting as a British children's writer, for *The Story of Doctor Dolittle* was first published in America and the award given to *The Voyages of Doctor Dolittle* was the Newbery, not the Carnegie Medal. But, as Edward Blishen has pointed out in his excellent Bodley Head monograph, Lofting not only retained his British citizenship throughout his life, but also remained in many ways essentially English. Nevertheless, the fact also remains that he lived all his working life in America and all his books were first published there. It is perhaps not an important debate; whatever nation claims Lofting he is one of the true internationals of children's writers, but it should be said that his work is included here for the pleasure of drawing attention to it rather than to claim it.

Edward Blishen's account of Lofting's saga of Doctor Dolittle is so good that it would be pointless to attempt to improve on it. He has made the essential points—that the

Drawing by Hugh Lofting for his book Doctor Dolittle's Post Office (*Cape*).

stories have a life of their own which grows and strengthens as the series develops; and that their great attraction lies in the combination of a consummate naturalness and a superb attention to detail. After the slightly false start of *The Story of Doctor Dolittle* everything that happens (once the basic suspension of disbelief has been achieved) has the logicality and inevitability of truth. If a man *could* talk to animals, and had the saint-like simplicity, complete unselfishness and insatiable curiosity of Dolittle, this, the reader feels, is how it would all have happened. This is how children reason, and this, no doubt, is why children all over the world have taken Dolittle to their hearts. The best of the stories are the five in the middle—*The Voyages, Post Office, Circus, Zoo* and *Caravan*. Thereafter the author's preoccupation with the horrors of war and man's perpetual egotism and greed becomes more obtrusive. It never completely darkens the picture, but it introduces an element that can disturb and perplex children and leads them to ask, worriedly, 'Why is it that the animals are always so much nicer than the humans?'

If it is true that the greatest writers in any field have always something of value to communicate, then Lofting must be one of the truly great writers for children, because his message of tolerance, generosity, and unselfish helpfulness to others shines through so clearly. As Blishen puts it 'it is never possible to forget, in enjoying the high spirits of his writing at its best, that it stands high above most other writing for children for having at its heart this profound concern for sane behaviour among living creatures'.

Few other pre-war writers equalled Nesbit or Lofting in sustained output. The best fantasies of the period were isolated books, such as Hilda Lewis's *The Ship That Flew*, an up-to-date and well-written version of *The Phoenix and the Carpet* idea that also inspired several other stories. Magic of various kinds informed most of the successful fantasies of this time. J. B. S. Haldane's *My Friend Mr Leakey* was an unusual book of short stories distinguished by an ingenious admixture of modern scientific knowledge and magic—science nowadays is so close to magic that it is surprising that more authors have not made use of it in this way.

The most successful of a number of books of convincing everyday magic was *The Magic Bedknob*, followed later by *Bonfires and Broomsticks*, by Mary Norton. The principal character is an otherwise conventional member of society, the leading light in village activities, who happens to be taking a correspondence course in witchcraft in her spare time, and the three children who discover her secret become most amusingly involved in the successes and failures of her spells. *The Magic Bedknob* was one of the best fantasies of the pre-war period and its author was to go on to even greater success later with *The Borrowers* (see p. 117). The two books were later combined in *Bedknob and Broomstick*.

The best, and most original of all the imaginative stories of the time, however, was J. R. R. Tolkien's *The Hobbit, or There and Back Again*. Like so many of the best books for children, *The Hobbit* was written after being told aloud to the author's own family, and both its prose and its occasional scraps of verse have that memorable quality that often distinguishes this kind of writing. Tolkien's creation of the Hobbits, and the unforgettable Gollum, did not come to full flower in this first book, but it was recognisably a contemporary masterpiece and it is to the credit of the critics of the day that a majority of them acknowledged it. The public, however, was slow to do so. They were not helped by one of the drabbest productions that has ever been given to so distinguished a book. Possibly its rather dreary appearance was the author's own choice, for it has not the air of a designed book. The author's illustrations have a curious quality, but are they not of a kind to fire the young reader's imagination and both *The Hobbit* and the greater fantasy that its author built from it, *The Lord of the Rings* (see p. 134), cry out for an inspired illustrator.

Two characteristically English books are 'BB's two stories about the last of the elves in Britain—*The Little Grey Men* and *Down the Bright Stream*. 'BB', who as D. J. Watkins-Pitchford was his own illustrator, impregnated these two pleasantly natural stories with a deep and sustaining love of the English countryside that gave them a distinction beyond their real merits as imaginative fiction; but the stories, although slight, have a quiet sincerity that makes them very pleasant reading.

Other unusual books worthy of mention were William Croft Dickinson's *The Eildon Tree*, one of the earliest time-shift stories, about two children who find themselves translated to thirteenth-century Scotland, and Richard Hughes's two volumes of short stories, *The Spider's Palace* and *Don't Blame Me*. Richard Hughes, whose *A High Wind in Jamaica* is one of the best modern stories *about* children, is a distinguished writer with a finely imaginative perception of the natural logic of children, and these two books of short stories contain some of the best things of their kind.

There was for a time a vogue for commissioning successful adult novelists to write occasional stories for children. Too often these suggested, as John Rowe Townsend has so aptly put it, 'the adult writer at play rather than the children's writer at work'[1] but a number of them were of interest for their humorously casual use of magic, as something which (far from being accompanied by the sound of other-worldly music and a 'most melodious twang') is really as logical and natural as the other odd things that go on around us. Eric Linklater wrote two such books, the first and better of which, *The Wind on the Moon*, was awarded the Carnegie Medal for 1944. There were the usual ingredients, the witch in the wood, the magic drink and the rest of it, but the author's riotous imagination, sense of fun and vivid writing combined to make a most entertaining story. Beverley Nichols's two children's books, *The Tree That Sat Down* and its sequel *The Stream That Stood Still*, were quieter and more carefully thought out, but like most modern fantasies had plenty of humour and their magic also was of a very practical and convincing kind.

Another established novelist who has written children's books, but with more serious intentions, is Rumer Godden. Her range is wide but the descriptive simplicity of her tales is best illustrated by *The Dolls' House*, a farthing novel that brilliantly succeeds in depicting adult situations and conflicts in a story that on the surface is no more than a simple tale about dolls. Many of her stories are told in this miniature form. There are others about dolls, and one, *The Mousewife*, derived from a note in Dorothy Wordsworth's Journal about the friendship between a caged dove and a mouse, that becomes, in Rumer Godden's hands, a parable about oppression.

Christianna Brand, another successful novelist, has also written two children's stories about *Nurse Matilda*. Matilda is a dumpy, black-clothed Victorian nurse, who materialises mysteriously when a family of children needs to be reformed. The story is apparently a family one, shared by the author and her illustrator, Edward Ardizzone, who has brought this irresistible period piece of Victoriana enchantingly to life, so although she has since written a sequel it is unlikely that she will write more creative books for children.

[1] John Rowe Townsend, *Written for Children*, Garnet Miller, 1965.

Considerable skill, and a genuine absorption in the doings of small children is needed to sustain successful stories for this level and the technical accomplishment of the better authors is apparent. Among a number of authors who have produced series of stories are Leila Berg, whose *The Adventures of Chunky* is a delightful near-relation to Professor Haldane's *My Friend Mr Leakey*; Joan Robinson, whose many adventures of *Teddy Robinson* seem irresistible to children at the right age; Helen Morgan, with her *Mrs Pinny* books, and Margaret Storey, with *The Smallest Doll*, *The Smallest Bridesmaid* and so on. Naughtiness and smallness seem to be two essential qualities in books of this kind, and one of the most successful of them all is *My Naughty Little Sister* by Dorothy Edwards. No parent should deny himself the pleasure of

Drawing by Shirley Hughes for When My Naughty Little Sister Was Good, *by Dorothy Edwards (Methuen).*

sharing Dorothy Edwards's book with his daughter, at any age from four to seven. Four to be read aloud to, seven to read for herself. Rather older children (and their parents) will enjoy the stories in Joan Aiken's collections, *All You've Ever Wanted*, *More Than You Bargained For*, and *A Necklace of Raindrops*.

Two survivors from an earlier period that appear to have retained their appeal are Pamela Travers's books about *Mary Poppins* and Katherine Tozer's about *Mumfie*. Mary Poppins, a nursemaid with magical powers of an unexpected kind, is a most endearing character, and Pamela Travers was extremely lucky in her illustrator, Mary Shepard, who caught to perfection the turned-up nose and consequential air that distinguish Mary Poppins from most other magical personalities. For she is inordinately vain, anything but good-tempered, and the justice she administers is of an incalculable kind, doled out by fits and starts in just such a way as no doubt the Olympian authority of more prosaic nannies must appear to children. She is an inspired conception, and the books in which she appears have a deserved place in the hearts of present-day children.

Katherine Tozer's Mumfie is a small toy elephant, and his adventures with his tall friend Scarecrow seem to be very popular with young children. Katherine Tozer illustrated the books herself, and the illustrations, which show Mumfie as a most appealing little character, undoubtedly had much to do with the success of the books, for there is nothing distinguished about the stories themselves, which are little more than lightly entertaining.

In similar vein are Michael Bond's series of books about the adventures of *Paddington*, a bear whose best intentions lead always to trouble. This is ideal fare for young children and has the added attraction of being satisfying to read aloud. Peggy Fortnum's illustrations add to the appeal of a pleasantly natural series.

There are many more good, or at least adequate, books for young children than have been dealt with here. This is a difficult group of books to assess by normal critical standards. Some of the best books are outstanding and these present few problems, but the majority are 'purpose' books, that have been written specifically with a particular age-level, or category, in mind, often to commissions. These can rarely be assessed by the same standards as can be applied to fiction for older readers, or even to fantasies and picture books. It is an

Drawing by Peggy Fortnum for A Bear Called Paddington, *by Michael Bond* (*Collins*).

often unsatisfactory middle ground that is as difficult for
critics as it is for authors—which is no doubt why most serious
critics avoid it. Here and there an exceptional book shines out,
even in the 'series', but in the main this is an age at which
children are easily satisfied, and thus likely to be fobbed off
with easy writing, which makes hard reading for adults.

No attempt, therefore, has been made to examine the books
in the innumerable series to select the better books among
them. This is an attempt to examine the best, not to draw
attention to every example of professional competence.
Nevertheless the existence of these books in series should be
mentioned because it is an interesting contemporary development which poses new problems for children's writers, who
are, as a result, subjected to temptations from which adult
novelists are spared.

Once an adult novelist has established a reputation he may
be subjected to pressures of many kinds. He may be asked to
write articles for periodicals on subjects which do not appeal

Drawing by Mary Shepard for Mary Poppins Comes
Back, *by P. L. Travers (Collins).*

to him (but for which the fees are tempting); to appear on television; to take part in panel games; to open Book Weeks; to do anything and everything in which his name may seem likely to attract an audience. But he is *not* asked to use the talent which made his reputation in the same way but at a lower level and for less intelligent readers. It is difficult to imagine even the most commercially-minded and enterprising publisher approaching a number of distinguished modern novelists—Angus Wilson, Iris Murdoch, or Anthony Powell, for example—and asking them to write 'an 8,000 word novel, with a simple plot, and easy language, for younger adults'. But this must happen constantly to any successful writer for children.

What has brought this about is the steady increase over the past twenty years, but especially in the last decade, in 'series'. There is nothing basically wrong about the conception of a series of approximately uniform books. In some fields, especially directly educational ones such as science, natural history, geography and so on, series can be of value, because the necessary discipline of length, treatment, proper presentation of illustrations, and series style—if imposed by a discriminating publisher and a good general editor—ensures that an honest and reliable standard is maintained. But the idea goes bad when it is applied to imaginative writing, at any level. Creative writing of any kind must come naturally from well-springs within the author and it is improbable that any deliberately created collection of stories, uniform in length and treatment but by a variety of authors, will produce writing of the first class. It may, and often does, produce adequate writing, in a recognisable set of books on which parents and other present-givers can rely if they are incapable of selecting for themselves, or unwilling to make the effort. But it rarely produces the best and it can hardly be good for writers of real quality to have to force their minds and talents back to this kind of writing *after* they have discovered the type of book they genuinely want to write and have learnt how to write it.

Unhappily, even this basic conception of the reliability of books in a series has now to some extent been vitiated by its commercial success. The series idea has been demonstrably profitable, so every publisher must have one and it has now become almost as difficult for parents to discriminate between series as it formerly was for them to do so between authors. A series produced by a reputable publisher can usually be relied on to contain honestly put together and morally impeccable narratives, even if it is unlikely to contain many works of real fire or imagination. But there are other series which cannot be relied on to do anything but make money for their publishers and, one hopes, their authors. When in doubt study the list of authors. There are a number of well-known, highly popular authors whose names are frequently used by publishers to bolster up an otherwise mediocre series list. A good publisher does not do this, and nor does a good author. There are exceptions, but not enough to disqualify the advice that a first-class author will rarely appear on the lists of more than one series. And there are also lesser authors whose names will be found regularly on such lists as known suppliers of standard series fodder. If a series has too many such names its general standard is predictable.

Drawing by Margery Gill for The Youngest Storybook,
compiled by Eileen Colwell (*The Bodley Head*).

IV. Fiction for Children

Writing in 1950 it was possible with some confidence to divide fiction for older children into a small number of convenient categories and to comment that it had 'on the whole followed conventional patterns and there had been few outstanding books'.

Twenty years later both classification and comment are completely out of date. It is a measure of the astonishing change that has taken place in writing for children over this period that this section should need such drastic revision. A few critical comments on major books survive. There are some permanencies even in this field. But the survey of trends and the general assessment of achievement has been overtaken by events. Mary Harris and a few other writers have brought new life and realism to that seemingly extinct species, the school story for girls; a completely new school of historical fiction has emerged; writers like William Mayne, Leon Garfield, John Rowe Townsend, Hester Burton, K. M. Peyton and Alan Garner have given new directions to the adventure story—for these *are* adventures, even though of a very different kind; realistic writing for children, though as yet the least successful of these new developments, is steadily improving—and how surprising today seems the 1950 comment that 'there is little fantasy written for older children'!

In a work that attempts to survey seventy years of writing for children, however, the books of the first half of the century still have to be assessed and the difference between the work of the two periods makes organisation of the material difficult. Furthermore, the problems that writers for children in the first half of the century had to solve were different from those facing present-day writers.

The difficulties that anyone setting out to write profession-ally for children in the first half of the century had to encounter were essentially practical. Unless an author had been pre-viously successful in some other field of writing, publishers were unwilling to accept anything that broke new ground, or was unusual in any way. Most authors in the late 'twenties and 'thirties had to limit themselves to conventional stories of various kinds—school stories, adventure stories, horse stories—and the writing of these was made increasingly difficult by the reduction in the age at which a particular type of book was read. Harvey Darton had already noted this trend, but it increased steadily throughout the century and by 1950 school and adventure stories which twenty years ago would have been read at fourteen or sixteen were being read at ten or even nine.

The problems posed by such a rapidly reducing age level to writers of children's fiction were obvious, and were partly responsible for the wild improbability of the plots of so many of the stories of the time. Children like to imagine themselves in the situations they are reading about, so authors were driven progressively to reduce the ages of their heroines and heroes, with results that put an impossible strain on credulity. For adventures which can by a stretch of imagination be con-ceived as just possible for a boy of sixteen become ludicrous for one of nine or ten.

Children had also in the first half of the century begun to read adult fiction much earlier, with the result that it largely replaced the better type of adventure story for boys which had been popular at the end of the last and the beginning of this century. Such writers as Rudyard Kipling, Arthur Conan Doyle, H. Rider Haggard, H. G. Wells, Stanley Weyman, John Buchan, Jeffrey Farnol, Henry Seton Merriman and Anthony Hope produced a type of story that was almost perfectly suited for school-age reading and so further reduced the market for the genuine children's book.

Children's fiction was thus read at an earlier age, and for a shorter time, and this reduction of both the range and extent of such reading brought about a drastic reduction in quality. The more intelligent a child is, the more likely he is to turn sooner to adult reading, unless the children's books with which he is provided give him something to get his intellectual teeth into, and stimulate his imagination. Publishers of the time would have been unlikely to accept any books capable of doing that, even if they had existed, so it is not surprising that fiction then consisted principally of books for children who were capable of appreciating only the simpler type of plot, with plenty of action, few demands on the intelligence, and virtually no characterisation—for it takes some imagination to be interested in other people's characters and the motives behind their actions. It is not difficult to produce simple action stories of the kind required at that time, but it is a tedious as well as a mercenary task and no writer of integrity could long tolerate it. The natural result was that the best writers of the period turned to producing books for the intelligent child at a younger age, leaving adventure stories and other fiction for older children to lesser writers.

A few authors overcame these difficulties and produced books that have stood the test of time, but the majority were produced by writers who were either under-paid hacks or over-paid formula-mongers. The commercial and practical difficulties of the period created an unfertile soil for the growth of the genuine writer for children.

In the second half of the century the situation completely changed. For reasons that have been briefly examined in the historical section it became profitable to publish a better type of children's book. For the first time writers for children found themselves in a position to pick and choose, to decide for themselves the kind of book they would like to write, to experiment with different kinds of writing for children. For a writer with any real talent the immediate financial difficulties were less, because his books were likely to be accepted promptly and to sell well. And he met less resistance from publishers to difficult and demanding books—some publishers even encouraged them.

The difficulties facing a writer for children in the 1970s are of a very different kind. If he is a writer of integrity—and the most encouraging and rewarding aspect of a study of contemporary children's books is the discovery that so many of them are by such writers—he will be increasingly concerned with problems that are intellectual, emotional, moral and social, rather than the practical ones that confronted his counterpart in the 1930s or '40s. He will find himself and his work being critically examined by all sorts of people who would previously have been unlikely to take writing for children seriously. Librarians, reviewers in distinguished periodicals, teachers, lecturers, even university professors, will all assess it and give judgement on it. He will be called to many different Bars to give an account of himself, and to explain why his books fail in this or that particular. He will discover (to his surprise and concern if he is one kind of writer, to his gratification if he is another) that his work is regarded as of great social and educational significance; that it is being taken seriously because of the effect it may have on the future development, intellectually and morally of his readers. He will be asked to address learned and consequential seminars on such topics as 'The Importance of Social Realism in Writing for Young Children', and may be surprised to discover that educational authorities are at last finding out for themselves something that everyone seriously interested in children's books has known for the past century—that the stories children read play a vital part in their total education. A part that may be at least as important as their formal studies.

It would be surprising if all this 'Parkinson for children' as Marcus Crouch called it in a *Times Literary Supplement* leading article, did not affect the writer's own attitude to his work. If he is a genuine one, with a sincere and conscientious approach to his task, he will already have questioned the value of it. He will have asked himself what he is seeking to achieve; whether he believes that children will really enjoy, benefit from, like, or even understand what he is trying to tell them. He will have tested his own views on morality, religion, right and wrong, evil, cruelty and pain—even, nowadays, sex—in relation to their effect on his young readers. He may even, without all this prodding and pushing from the well-intentioned, *want* to make children experience the suffering caused by prejudice, hate, meanness and stupidity. If he is that sort of writer the present state of critical opinion and debate may perhaps do him no harm. It may even help him, by sharpening his own attitudes, pointing out new evils to be explored, new prejudices to be exploited.

But there are other kinds of writers for children, who do not need to be directed into such service; who, if left alone, are capable of writing books that will achieve the same results, but without the shadowy sombreness that are beginning to darken much of contemporary fiction for children. Hugh Lofting succeeded in making many perfectly explicit statements about selfishness, prejudice and cruelty in a series of books that never lost their natural gaiety. Rumer Godden succeeded in the even more unlikely feat of communicating a surprising amount about human nature and the drama and tragedy of adult life, in stories about dolls. It is not necessary to make a great show of seriousness to be serious, and the stories most likely to help children to a better understanding of life and the strangely-constructed human beings with whom they will have to share it, are often those least obviously designed to do so.

How one wishes that the writer who is capable of achieving those rare moments of warmth and delighted recognition, of sudden awarenesses and pricking tears—the children's book equivalents of the shiver down the spine, or the hair standing on end that great poetry arouses—could be left alone to do what he best knows how to do! Unhappily it is unlikely that he will be.

For one of the major problems facing the contemporary writer for children is to resist the pressures that will be put on him to write in currently fashionable ways, even if those ways do not come naturally to him. And, above all, to avoid the temptation to take himself too seriously. Some notable practitioners in this field write about their work as if they were Dostoevsky, and several good critics have recently drawn attention to the fact that too many contemporary writers for children appear to be more interested in themselves than in their readers. The best writing for children is a self-effacing exercise in shared enjoyment and writers who forget their readers soon lose them. And, as discussion of the various categories of fiction will, I hope, demonstrate, the best books are still about people. Those familiar themes of good and evil, jealousy and treachery, love and hate (about none of which is there anything at all new) will be there, but only in their normal place as an inevitable part of life. The real substance of any good book comes from the people in it; what they are like, whether they can be changed by events, and what happens to them.

For reasons explained above it would be impracticable to consider the great mass of fiction involved strictly chronologically. Both topical and chronological treatments have their attractions, but the historical section has to some extent shown the general development of all kinds of children's books over the period, and there are so many books to be considered, with so much overlapping of topics and writers, that a purely historical treatment would become both unwieldy and unnecessarily complex. The topical treatment used in the first edition has, therefore, been preserved, but with side glances at other sections where this is necessary to establish common ground.

School Stories

The school story was always an artificial type and its decline towards the middle of the century was neither unexpected nor deplored. Talbot Baines Reed, in *The Cock House at Fellsgarth* and *The Fifth Form at St Dominic's*, brought the type to a perfection of unreality that later writers could only copy. Kipling introduced new ideas in *Stalky & Co.*, but these were not of a kind that practitioners in the older form could follow. A few, of whom Gunby Hadath and Hylton Cleaver were the most successful, tried to continue the familiar pattern by superimposing a more modern façade (one of Hadath's later books dealt with the entry of grant-aided boys into public schools) but the unreality of the genre became increasingly apparent and by 1950 there were few boys' boarding-school stories of the old pattern still in print.

A development which could perhaps be traced to *Stalky and Co.* was the emergence of stories of schooldays of an altogether different type, written as it were from outside the school gates rather than from within, and not primarily for children—certainly not for the children who read the old kind of school stories. Horace Annesley Vachell's *The Hill*, E. F. Benson's *David Blaize* and Hugh Walpole's *Jeremy* books were one side of this development. The other was represented by Arnold Lunn's *The Harrovians*, Alec Waugh's *The Loom of Youth*, Beverley Nichols's *Prelude* and many others, none of which has very much to do with children's books, except in so far as they may have represented a reaction on the part of novelists against the 'boys' school story' attitude to life at school.

Although the traditional boys' school story was virtually extinct by 1950, stories about school continued to be written and one of the best children's books of the past twenty years is in fact a school story—though probably few readers think of it that way.

William Mayne's *A Swarm in May* is a minor masterpiece; a superb piece of imagination brilliantly executed, with a rare quality which lifts it from the common level of children's books into that limited class of books that are simply books to

Drawing by C. Walter Hodges for A Swarm in May, *by William Mayne (Oxford University Press).*

be read and enjoyed at any level, by anyone who is capable of appreciating the best of its kind. Contentious as the critical scene may have become, and divided though opinions may be on so many topics affecting children's books, there are few critics who would deny *A Swarm in May* its rightful place as one of the twentieth century's best children's books. But it *is*, nevertheless, a school story. A choir school is an unusual setting, and the boys and masters are themselves anything but usual, but everything rings true and much of the success of the book derives from its lovingly observed picture of a close community. The later books, *Choristers' Cake, Cathedral Wednesday* and *Words and Music*, lack the unusual and moving theme of *A Swarm in May* and are, as a result, nearer to conventional school stories, but from any other writer they too would be outstanding.

But this is only a passing reference to William Mayne, whose work as a whole will be considered later (see p. 138).

Some conventional boys' school stories continued to appear and a number of writers have done their best to introduce new elements, as Gunby Hadath and others had done thirty years earlier, by setting their stories in modern schools. E. W. Hildick's stories about *Jim Starling*, for example, are a praiseworthy attempt to deal honestly and realistically with a working-class school from a boy's point of view and Anthony Buckeridge's *Jennings* books have more humour and better, though limited, observation of character than most contemporary stories of their kind. Their success is probably due to the combination of a kind of slap-dash fun with a racy use of contemporary slang, and this has its dangers for a writer. Nothing dates faster than primary school slang and (as Margery Fisher has suggested in *Intent upon Reading*) one of the reasons for the survival of Talbot Baines Reed's books long after their fellows is probably the fact that he used relatively little slang and his dialogue therefore did not date so rapidly.

There are other writers of conventional school stories for boys, but it would be pointless to list them here. The majority of such books still suffer from the defects of any deliberately contrived type. They are written for the immediate moment, will serve their purpose for a time and then some other writer of the same kind of thing, but with an outlook ten years younger, will take their place.

Books will still be written in which children are at school for the whole or part of the story, but these will be no different in kind from any other story of everyday life. The boys' school story was always an artificial category and children's books will be better without it. As an American correspondent pointed out in a series of letters in *The Times Literary Supplement* about modern children's fiction, one of the reasons why children's literature has not in the past been taken seriously by critics is because it has never been seen as a literary form. It has always been seen as a commercial category, like the Detective story, the Western, the Romantic Love story, and so on. An inevitable product of that commercialisation was the further division into readily saleable products—the School Story, the Adventure Story, the Family Story, the Horse Story, and so on. That such categories should still exist is a survival from the 'reward' days—one wonders if books can still be found piled up on wholesalers' tables as they used to be in my day, with notices reading 'Adventure Stories at 1/–', 'Boys' School Stories at 1/6', 'Girls' School Stories at 1/–', 'Horse Stories at 2/–' (Horse Stories tended always to be slightly more expensive; a nice exercise in unconscious snobbery?).

Most adult readers seem not to experience much difficulty in selecting their books without such artificial divisions. In a good modern library the tendency nowadays is for all fiction to be in a single alphabetical order, including even categories like detective stories and science fiction which might earlier have been separated or distinguished by symbols. The argument applied to adult books, that all books are measurable as good, bad or indifferent by the same standards irrespective of their categories, is equally applicable to children's books. The sooner it becomes possible to consider a book for children on its own merits, without having to think of it as belonging to a particular category, the better it will be for everyone; writers, critics—and children.

Division by topic may be unavoidable for a time in histori-cal discussions of the development of children's books, but by the end of the century anyone writing a book like this should be able to write of children's books as a single field, just as an adult critic writes of the novel. The writers themselves are likely to make this unavoidable, because they seem no longer prepared to remain in little boxes. Writers like William Mayne are unclassifiable—school stories? fantasy? adventure stories?—and increasingly writers for children are likely to extend their range by writing as they choose, over the whole field of children's reading.

Girls' school stories came on to the scene later, but have followed much the same pattern of development as the boys' school stories, of an emancipation from formulas towards a new freedom. The principal girls' school story writers in the first half of the century were Angela Brazil, Elinor Brent-Dyer, Dorita Fairlie Bruce and Elsie J. Oxenham. All be-longed to this century and although Angela Brazil died in 1947 the others went on publishing for some time after that date and some of their books are still in print. Each was responsible for several series of books about the same characters or school, of which Elinor Brent-Dyer's *Chalet School* series was the farthest removed from reality and Dorita Fairlie Bruce's *Dimsie* series the nearest to it. But none bore much relation to twentieth-century school life and despite an occasional flash of vitality like Nancy Breary's *No Peace for the Prefects*, by 1950 the girls' boarding school story seemed well on the way to extinction.

But school is, after all, an important part of every child's life, so it ought not to have been so surprising as it seemed at the time when a completely new kind of girls' school story began to appear. A number of writers seem to have been groping towards the same conception at about the same time, but the development can be observed at work most directly in the books of Mary K. Harris, whose *Seraphina*, written in 1960, is one of the best stories about girls at home and at school that has yet been written. Her first book, *Gretel at St Brides*, was published in 1941 and might well have been written by any of the writers listed in the previous paragraph. *The Wolf* (1946) was not a school story, but she returned to the theme in 1953 with *Henrietta at St Hilary's*. Her earlier books were published by conventional 'reward' publishers, and looked exactly like all the other girls' school stories of their time. It is possible, re-reading them now with hindsight, to see traces of what was to come, but she remained unrecognized until the publication in 1958, by a different publisher, of *Emily and the Headmistress*. This low-key story of a little girl left alone at school during her mother's absence is a completely satisfactory piece of writing, almost beyond criticism. There are some nice points of detail, all the characters are well observed, and no normal reader can avoid becoming warmly involved in Emily's affairs. But Mary Harris's talent came to its full flower in *Seraphina*. This is a real novel, with an excellent plot, characters observed in reasonable depth, and a convincing development. For the first time the school story (if this *is* a school story and not just a realistic story for girls that happens to have some school life in it) had been freed from conservatism, snobbery, 'play girls play', contempt for work, and all the other things for which the traditional school story had rightly been criticized. Two later books, *Penny's Way* and *The Bus Girls*, are memorable for their sketches of a couple of ordinary mothers. She wrote only one other book, *Jessica on Her Own*, before she died in 1966. Her work is at least as good as that of many writers who have won the Carnegie Medal and better than some. One wonders whether a subconscious prejudice against the school story may have influenced the librarian judges against awarding it to her in 1960 for *Seraphina*?

Antonia Forest's stories of the Marlow family contain an almost equally new and realistic treatment of the school story. *Autumn Term*, published in 1948, was in fact ahead of Mary Harris's better books in date of publication, but the unusual reality of her stories remained unnoticed until her second book, *End of Term*, was published in 1959. Opinions differ about relative merits. There is a coolness and a sense of withdrawal about her books which prevent the reader from becoming as involved with Nicola, as for example, with Mary Harris's Emily, and her plots seem sometimes a little muddled to readers coming fresh to them without the detailed knowledge of the Marlow family that devoted readers have. But her books brought a vitality and a crisp freshness to school stories which was completely new.

As has been said earlier, there will always be stories about school, because being taught, the teachers who do it, the buildings in which it is done, and the other children they meet there, are a vital part of children's lives during the very years in which they are reading children's books. But home is an equally important part of life in those years and the future of the school story lies probably with a new kind of book that combines both. Mary Harris's *Penny's Way* does this very successfully and a number of other writers seem to have been experimenting, consciously or unconsciously, along these lines. A good example of the genre is Margaret Storey's *Pauline*. In most books of this kind the interplay between school and home is uneasily, and sometimes uncomfortably, balanced, one being the real focus of the story and the other simply an adjunct. But in *Pauline* both are essential because the tensions in Pauline's life at home, when her father dies and she has to go unwillingly to live with relatives whom she does not like, are made worse by her association with friends made at school and later resolved after she has run away with one of them. There is none of the too obvious gulf that separates school and home in the stereotype school story and both halves of Pauline's life are made equally important and equally interesting.

William Mayne is another writer who is able to combine school and home very effectively. *A Swarm in May* was considered earlier, in the section on boys' school stories, because that is purely about life in a school. But when he is writing about boys in a different environment he clearly sees no division between home and school. Boys (and girls) move freely from one to the other and teacher and parent, home life and school life run concurrently, as they should. The balance is perhaps not quite so even as it is in *Pauline*, because with most of Mayne's books it is the other life than home which is the more important part of the story, but the home life is equally well observed and equally genuine. A story like *Sand*, for example, is an almost perfect example of this fusion. Boys' school and girls' school, home life and leisure life, all play their parts in the development of the story. But I do not want to analyse William Mayne's work too closely here because that is considered as a whole in a later section. It has only been mentioned to make the point that this fusion between home and school in a new kind of story is taking place with both girls' and boys' school stories.

Stories of Adventure

The boys' adventure story very nearly went the way of the school story. No writers for the first half of the century came near the stature of such nineteenth-century giants as Henty, Ballantyne, and Manville Fenn. A few writers, of whom the best known were Herbert Strang and Percy F. Westerman, continued to write full-blooded adventure stories on the old patterns, with a sufficiency of moral purpose, but a steady deterioration, which was accelerated by the war, nevertheless became apparent.

The general scheme of such stories was usually the triumph of a typically British hero over evil-doers of one kind or another, but their development was marred by an ever increasing improbability and a tendency to introduce more and more violence in action in order to overcome the flatness of the writing and to disguise the writer's inadequacy.

The genre became a factory product and largely ceased to attract writers of distinction. It became, instead, one of the principal fields for professional children's writers, some of whom established considerable reputations. The best known author in the field was W. E. Johns, whose series of stories about the air adventures of his famous character *Biggles* approximated most closely to the old pattern. Biggles, however, was a man, not a boy, and his adventures took place principally among adults. The later tendency was for the central characters to be a boy, or a girl, and for the subsidiary adult characters who used to assist the quick-witted youth (as in the *Treasure Island* tradition) gradually to disappear.

It became a commonplace occurrence in such fiction to find young children outwitting, and often overcoming by physical violence, gangs of hardened criminals without any adult assistance whatsoever. As a distinguished children's librarian, Eileen Colwell, commented drily when reviewing a book of this type by the best-selling children's writer of the time, Enid Blyton, 'but what chance has a gang of desperate criminals against three small children!' Never were so many fully armed blackguards so easily overcome by so few children; never were adults so incompetent or adolescents so invincible;

never were boys so brave or girls so gaily indifferent to danger; never, alas, were parents so entirely non-existent or children so much encouraged to enter a world of fantastic wish-fulfilment.

A few writers attempted to improve the pattern by introducing some extraneous and more uplifting element. Malcolm Saville, for example, contrived to impart an atmosphere of the English countryside to his otherwise typical adventure stories, and Peter Dawlish and other writers gave their tales an authentic nautical background. But from the moment when the mysterious stranger arrived in the village, or the muffled conversation which first gave news of the inevitable 'treasure' was overheard in a train on the way to the summer holiday, they reverted to pattern.

Disturbed by the increasing unreality of these stories one publisher, Basil Blackwell, who had earlier tried to raise the standard of 'annuals' by his *Joy Street* books, in the middle of the period produced a series of *Tales of Action* by distinguished contemporary writers which attempted to combine the thrills required (for it seemed at that time that the contemporary child would accept no substitute for excitement) with real characterization and good writing. The editor of the series was L. A. G. Strong, a successful adult novelist who produced, in *King Richard's Land*, *The Fifth of November*, and *Mr Sheridan's Umbrella*, three sincerely written and carefully constructed stories for boys. Cecil Day Lewis wrote *Dick Willoughby* and Rex Warner *The Kite* for the same series. Another contributor to the series was Geoffrey Trease, who became one of the few children's writers of the time to take the adventure story seriously. His stories were usually based on history, but differed from most historical stories for children in taking an unusual viewpoint and attempting always a genuinely objective treatment. Thus in *Grey Adventurer* the hero is a Puritan and the Cavaliers anything but heroes; in *Cue for Treason* the enclosure of the commons is seen from the farmers' viewpoint, not the landlord's, and *Comrades of the Charter* tells the story of the Chartist rising not as an occasion for adventure on the part of a well-to-do hero, but from within, describing how the rebellion was planned and why it failed. But Trease was almost alone in applying an adult standard of criticism to the adventure story, and he was unique in attempting to make children politically conscious by explaining in his stories the causes of social unrest.

Drawing by Brian Wildsmith for Follow My Black
Plume, *by Geoffrey Trease (Macmillan).*

A feature of the period was the infiltration of the most
significant aspects of the contemporary adventure story—
preoccupation with criminal activities—into other fields.
No story of school life was complete without its smugglers,
hunters of buried treasure, or black marketeers, to pep up
the once sufficiently satisfying inter-House rivalries, cricket
matches, and midnight feasts, and the same became true of
the story of everyday life, which proved, however, better
able to resist the invasion than other types. The better
stories of this kind managed to avoid the more obvious
dangers, and the best of them contrived to extract excitement
from the absorbing events in the ordinary lives of children.

The first Arthur Ransome story, *Swallows and Amazons*,
was published in 1931. It was something completely new.
So many imitations have since appeared that it is difficult for
us today to remember how new and exciting that first book
was. Ransome's contribution to the development of the
modern children's story is not always sufficiently realized.
It is a common-place, nowadays, to say that 'Ransome

invented holidays', or 'Ransome invented the sailing adventure story', or 'Ransome invented the story about the country', or 'Ransome first set children free from parents'; all these statements are true enough, but they miss the essential point of his contribution to children's writing.

I imagine that, in fact, he consciously invented very little. What he did do, almost for the first time since *Bevis*, was to write a completely truthful book based on his own experiences with youthful, like-minded friends camping and sailing in the Lake District. Probably the idea of inventing any new type of children's story never entered his head until afterwards. The important thing was that he had observed, understood and shared satisfactions with groups of children who enjoyed a way of life that happened to appeal to him. He had studied them with that delighted affectionate enjoyment Jane Austen derived from her own circle, and when the idea came to him to write a book for children his aim was not to invent fantastic adventures but to get as close as he could to the truth. It would be, of course, imaginative rather than real truth. Like all true artists, he supplied here and there the interpretative touch that gives cohesion and significance to the story, but he permitted himself no extravagances and none of his children ever for a moment acts or speaks out of character.

Ransome carried his passion for accuracy and probability to unusual lengths—even going so far as to let himself drift across the North Sea in a small yacht to test the plot of one of his later books—and the practicalities that he introduced can be tried and tested at every point. Even the illustrations are unusual, for Ransome, despairing of finding an artist who would take the trouble to be completely accurate and after an artist had failed to satisfy him, re-illustrated the first book himself and continued to illustrate the remainder of the series. His books, which began with *Swallows and Amazons* and continued with *Swallowdale* and others at regular intervals of two years, are not sequels in the accepted sense, nor do they constitute a series, but they are all about the same group of children and their friends, who grow older naturally throughout the books (no perpetual youth for Ransome). Most, though not all, of their adventures take place on or near water, and a boy or girl who has read the whole series must have a pretty thorough knowledge of small boat sailing; but there are a hundred and one other hints in his books of things to do and how to do them, for Ransome contrives to

Drawing by Arthur Ransome for his book Peter Duck
(*Cape*).

get his excitement from probabilities and his suspense from the success or failure of child or adult in perfectly possible activities. One of his best stories, *Pigeon Post*, which was awarded the first Carnegie Medal in 1936, is a perfect model of how to write a children's story, for in it he subjects his group of children to all the superficial ingredients of the conventional children's 'thriller'. There is a mysterious stranger, a search for treasure, midnight excursions, and so on; but how skilfully it is all handled and how differently the children themselves react! And yet how much more truly exciting it is than the average adventure story containing the same ingredients superficially handled.

Ransome's contribution to the twentieth-century children's story was incalculable. He led the way to a more natural approach; to a realistic and unsentimental characterization; to completely true to life dialogue, and to a new conception of the kind of excitement necessary to keep children reading for pleasure. He has had, of course, a host of imitators. He launched a whole fleet of sailing adventure stories; he started the immense flood of stories about the summer holidays; he began the fashion for books with plenty of country lore in them. But above all the success of his books showed both authors and publishers that it was possible for a successful book to break away from the 'reward' pattern.

Arthur Ransome's influence could be seen in the majority of writers for children since 1931, but he had in addition some direct followers. The most successful of these were Katherine Hull and Pamela Whitlock. When they were fifteen or so these two loved Ransome's books so much that when they had read all that he had then published they decided to write another for themselves. The result was *The Far Distant Oxus*, a story about riding and camping on Exmoor that was an immediate success because it had, in addition to all the usual Ransome ingredients, the added delight of ponies. *Escape to Persia* and *The Oxus in Summer* were sequels in the same manner.

Arthur Ransome's work has been considered under adventure stories because that was how it was seen at the time and it played an essential part in the development of these stories. Just as William Mayne and Mary Harris showed that stories about life at school need not be 'school stories', so Ransome began the movement away from the 'adventure story' as a stylized form towards a new kind of children's book that was simply about the adventure of living.

Drawing by Pamela Whitlock for her book The Far-Distant Oxus, *written with Katharine Hull* (*Cape*).

One of the early writers to follow this lead was Noel Streatfeild. No crooks and few villains figure in her stories, which are nevertheless absorbing. She wrote with intimate knowledge of the background of each of her stories and filled them with real people whose characters were accurately observed and portrayed. Above all she understood instinctively the real interests and enthusiasms of modern children. Not all her books were of the 'career' type, but her reputation was built up by a series of such books: *Ballet Shoes*, *The Circus is Coming* (which won the Carnegie Medal for 1938), *Curtain Up* and *Tennis Shoes*.

Kitty Barne, another Carnegie Medal winner, was also interested in real-life careers and *She Shall Have Music*, *Family Footlights*, and *Musical Honours* all dealt with the practicalities of artistic jobs. Her medal winner, *Visitors from London*, described the experiences of a family of children with evacuees from London in the first summer of the war.

Other writers moved away from the traditional adventure story with varying degrees of success. Richard Armstrong and Peter Dawlish produced honestly observed and competently written stories of the sea, and Cecil Day Lewis, in *The Otterbury Incident*, tried to bring some reality into a gay story derived from the film *Nous Les Gosses* but concocted from the standard small boys-against-criminals plot. Other writers attempted to introduce more excitement in family stories. But times were changing and the 1950s saw the beginning of a newer kind of book, which is worthy of a better name than 'adventure story'.

It is not quite true to say that the traditional story of adventure has completely disappeared, because a few authors have produced books that are infinitely more realistic although they approximate to the older pattern in the concessions they make to the demands for excitement and thrills. The best of these are Allan Campbell McLean, with his John Buchan-ish stories of villainy of various kinds on the

Drawing by Richard Kennedy for The Key, *by Eilís Dillon* (*Faber*).

Island of Skye, *The Hill of the Red Fox*, *The Man of the House*, *Master of Morgana* and others; and Eilís Dillon with her very much better equivalents set on the west coast of Ireland, *The House on the Shore*, *The Island of Horses*, *The Singing Cave* and others. Eilís Dillon is an experienced novelist, so it is not surprising that her wide range of characters should all be fully drawn—the adults as well as the children. Both these authors succeed in communicating a real sense of setting and atmosphere and their characters, unlike their puppet equivalents in Biggles and his kind, are real people acting from believable motives. If the traditional adventure story has any future this is how it should be written.

But the difficulties facing the writer of adventure stories for boys are likely to increase and it is difficult to see much future for them. This is the field in which the problems of reducing age level and the introduction of adult fiction are felt most. Ransome and his followers wrote for a middle age between childhood and adolescence, but their books have moved backwards. They are now read much earlier, probably on the average between nine and eleven, certainly not later. The age at which boys begin reading adult thrillers is steadily reducing. Writers like Hammond Innes and Alastair MacLean are as easy to read as any boys' books and more exciting than most—and they do not carry the stigma of being 'children's books'. Most school libraries have copies and boys find them very early. Certainly not later than fourteen and with many boys much earlier.

The adventure story writer is unlikely, therefore, to have more than two or three years of reading to cater for. It is a narrow gap to fill, and one that is still contracting. And it is doubtful whether the kind of boy who demands exciting reading will continue to read children's books at any age, competing as they are with headier temptations of the kind symbolized by the James Bond stories, though even these are now being challenged.

The difficulties of the adventure story writer pose in its simplest form the essential problem facing children's books—the increasing sophistication of their readers. Much as one may disagree with what McLuhan deduces from his observations, he is right when he says that the present generation of children is completely different from any previous one. The intrusion into all our lives of the mass media in their various forms, but especially television, has made children much more aware of adult life. They know much more about how adults really think and act, about what really goes on in the adult world, than any previous generation of children. One of the most noticeable things about them, to an observant parent or anyone genuinely interested in children, is their keen awareness of *people*. They are interested, in a way that I have no recollection of having myself experienced until much later in life, in the way people behave and the reasons for their actions. They are not interested in a great depth, and are in fact easily bored by any too introspective examination of motives, but they seem genuinely to want to *know*.

The kind of stories that they prefer to read, therefore, in the ever-reducing period during which they are still prepared to read children's books, are unlikely to be traditional adventure stories—instead they will go, sooner and sooner, to MacLean, Innes, Fleming and the various kinds of undemanding adult fiction. In other words, for that intermediate mind-switched-off kind of escapist reading for which we all feel the need at some time in our lives, they will turn to adult books, because they do it better and are just as easy to read.

This is too large a topic for full examination here but, sketching possibilities in lightly, it seems probable that children's books will eventually be read in three main groups only. First picture and 'read aloud' books for the very young before they are able to read; then the intermediate picture story and first reading books; and finally the 'young novel', a comprehensive category of fiction for the severely limited period during which children are still prepared to read books specially produced for them ending, probably, not later than fourteen. The better authors who have come into prominence in the past twenty years seem to have foreseen such a development and are writing books that might have been expressly designed for such a period. Not surprisingly they tend to be unclassifiable.

Leon Garfield is one author who has invented what is almost a new category of his own to fill this need. His books are not historical novels—though they are set in the past—nor are they simply adventure stories—it is even possible to see them, in some lights, as fantasies. But they are more likely to be read and enjoyed by those who like stories with plenty of action and excitement, than by lovers of historical stories or fantasy and it seems logical, therefore, to consider them here.

Although Leon Garfield's work has strengthened with

each book, his manner and method has remained unchanged and it is impossible to mistake any book by Garfield for one by any other writer. They are all set in a not too precisely defined part of the eighteenth century; a period which seems to have been chosen more for the opportunities it presents than for any special reason of historical interest or research. It is not an imaginary period, in the sense that Joan Aiken's settings are imaginary, (see p. 122) but no serious attempt is made at historical accuracy. No doubt some reading must have been done to get the general picture of the period into the author's mind, but it would not be the kind of research that a Rosemary Sutcliff or a Stephanie Plowman undertakes before writing a historical novel and there are, as a result, occasional anachronisms and inaccuracies. But these are minor blemishes and it is clearly not Leon Garfield's intention to aim at an accurate historical picture. He has described his own method well:

> ... to me the eighteenth century—or my idea of it—is more of a locality than a time. And in this curious locality I find that I can represent quite contemporary characters more vividly than I could otherwise. It seems to work in rather a strange way. For example, when you see someone you know intimately in new clothes or even fancy dress, quite suddenly and fleetingly you see a fresher aspect of them. You see them stand out from the background that familiarity has consigned them to. For that brief moment they are no longer the comfortable furniture of your mind—the animated gown or suit— but something new and strange, yet at the same time something you know quite well.
> ... I admit I find the social aspects of contemporary life too fleeting to grasp imaginatively before they are legislated out of existence. And anyway, I don't think the novel is as suited to coping with them as is the television documentary or the newspaper. It was once, but not now. In the old days it was fine to take up arms in a social cause. But nowadays you are apt to find—thanks to some searching television series—that by the time your book is in print your shining weapons have a quaint and antique air, rather like a flypaper in a world of aerosols. From this point of view a story set two hundred years ago has an enormous advantage ... Fortunately for the novelist, human nature is more constant than fashion.

This is a convincing account of a novelist's method, interesting in a number of different ways, and the whole paper from which it is taken ('Writing for Children' in the second issue of *Children's Literature in Education*) is illuminating, both about the author's own method and about the whole problem of writing for children in the late twentieth century.

Leon Garfield's first book was *Jack Holborn*. It is the story of a foundling boy in search of his identity, told with fine gusto and decked out with a wealth of eighteenth-century trappings. The author has given a detailed account of the writing of this book (in the paper already referred to) and in this he confirms the story that it was first written, and submitted to a publisher, as an adult book, but that—

> it lacked certain qualities that have come to be expected in an adult book. At the same time it possessed certain qualities that were not suited to a juvenile book. It was far too long and it had too many passages of reflection on self-explanatory action.

Jack Holborn was drastically cut and revised, under the guidance of an experienced editor, and was an immediate success, the unusual quality of the author being unmistakable. But the fact that this first book finally came into existence as the result of an editorial exercise and an obviously successful co-operation between author and editor is illuminating and no doubt partly explains the curious feeling that his books give to some readers that they are being stage-managed.

Leon Garfield's second book, *Devil-in-the-Fog*, is not his best book, but it is an excellent example of the author's manner and serves as a good introduction to his work. If the reader likes this he will like all the author's work, if he dislikes it he will probably dislike them all. It is the story of George Treet, the eldest son of a family of strolling players, who learns suddenly that he may be the son of a nobleman and the heir to great wealth. He is taken into Sir John Dexter's family, to find Sir John mysteriously wounded, Lady Dexter cold, haughty and withdrawn and a family of rivals seemingly as vicious as they are jealous. Eventually, after a series of events which read better in the book than they would if described here, he discovers that he is Thomas Treet's son after all, that his supposed father Sir John Dexter has been the villain of the piece, and that the rivals are not so bad as he had thought. *Devil-in-the-Fog* is as stagey, theatrical and melodramatic as Treet's own performances no doubt were. The style of writing is high-pitched, inflated, with all the marks of the kind of historical writing which earlier had brought historical novels into disrepute. One almost expects a character to burst out with 'Gadzooks!' at any moment, and there are as many exclamation marks, leaders, and dashes as there ever were in Herbert Strang—

'My father is put in the stocks again! The injustice of it! My father is a genius—as are all of we Treets. A grand man, as great in mind as he is in body, for he's a large man who bears himself with more dignity than all the Justices in Kent put together. Except when the Stranger calls; and then his spirit seems to flicker and sink some-what . . . as if the Stranger was something dark and devilish and there was an unwholesome bargain eating away at my father's soul. . . .'

'I considered my last hour not only come but on the point of being gone. I considered Mrs Montague to be the most monstrous soul this side of Hell; and with a fair claim to the same distinction on the other side of it! . . . '

'Ah! Boy! Good, good! There he is! Shoot, boy—shoot before he 'scapes! Quick, boy! Kill him! Aim, boy! Hold the weapon up! To your eye! Kiss the hammer, boy! Then fire! Fire, boy! Fire! I command you to fire!'

Yet despite all this the book succeeds with most readers, who are carried along by the impetuosity and verve of the author's writing and attracted by the very theatricality and staginess of the period atmosphere which other readers find overdone. Much of the success of this creation of atmosphere must go to the illustrator, Antony Maitland. Garfield is better at creating an impressionistic atmosphere from his writing than he is at describing an actual scene and the fact that the reader is made vividly aware of what the author is seeking to project is at least as much due to the artist as it is to the author. One glance at the brilliantly coloured jacket of *Devil-in-the-Fog* and the reader knows immediately what kind of a book it is and what to expect from the characters in it.

The book in which Leon Garfield comes nearest to making

British Children's Books in the Twentieth Century

a complete success of the unique mixture of sinister characters, complex, sometimes obscure plots and macabre set-pieces that he has made peculiarly his own, is *Black Jack*. A foully unpleasant highwayman has saved himself from death at the hands of the hangman by secreting a silver tube in his throat. His body is taken from the gallows by a bodysnatcher, who has enlisted the help of a passing boy because Black Jack is so huge that he is too heavy for her to move. The boy is left alone unwillingly with the body; Black Jack comes to, makes off and forces the boy Bartholomew, to accompany him. On the road Black Jack resumes his old occupation. In one of the coaches which he waylays is Belle, the temporarily deranged daughter of a wealthy family, being taken to a private lunatic asylum. She escapes; Bartholomew, by now re-named Tolly, finds her and they are befriended by a seller of home-made panaceas who is the leader of a travelling fair. Black Jack rejoins Tolly because he has accidentally learnt that there is a reward for Belle's recovery and combines with a particularly loathsome boy, Hatch, to frustrate Tolly's efforts to preserve and cure Belle. The remainder of the story is concerned with the parallel threads of Hatch's efforts to profit from the situation (which are complicated by Black Jack's gradual conversion) and of Tolly's and Belle's growing love and her recovery. Hatch blackmails both the lunatic asylum proprietor and Belle's father, whom he finally murders. Belle is persuaded that her father committed suicide and that therefore she must be tainted after all, and goes voluntarily to the asylum. Black Jack helps Tolly to rescue her; they enlist the help of the original bodysnatcher to trace the surgeon to whom she sold Belle's father's body, and learn that he did not commit suicide but was shot in the back. London is in chaos caused by an earthquake and through this Black Jack, Tolly and Belle struggle down to Greenwich, where they are able to get aboard a ship owned by Tolly's uncle and escape. Hatch is drowned somewhere in the mêlée, and Black Jack, having put Belle and Tolly safely aboard, is left to fade away, possibly, but not very convincingly, to a better life.

It would be difficult to imagine a more unlikely story. Yet Leon Garfield makes it not only readable, but compulsively so by the pace and tension of his writing and the almost frenzied 'come along quickly, let's get on with action and not bother too much about what is really supposed to be going on' that is the special mark of his manner.

102

Drawing by Antony Maitland for Smith, *by Leon Garfield*
(Longman).

His third book, *Smith*, is probably his best known, and is
the one that has attracted most critical attention. It is a
closely woven pastiche of the darker side of eighteenth-
century London, with thieves' kitchens, pickpockets, hangings,
the Old Bailey, Newgate, pox and plague all brought together in a witches brew of a book that seems to have about
it the smell and sounds of the city that Garfield sees and to
have hanging over it the darkness and fog and dirtiness that
was at least one feature of the times. It is in many ways more

like a miniature, and of course infinitely lesser, novel by Dickens than a children's book but there is no doubt at all that many children do read this, and all his books, with zest and find them both exciting and stimulating. His most recent book, *The Drummer Boy*, carries his strange tales even farther along the road to confusion. It is full of things that no other living author for children could achieve, but it would be an intelligent child indeed who could follow the author's tortuous threads to the true centre of his maze. Much as one has to admire his set pieces, and some excellent humorous writing, there is too much in this book that strikes false notes and too much that will mystify, confuse and unnecessarily distress young readers for it to be completely satisfying. Whatever may be true of *Jack Holborn*, *Devil-in-the-Fog* or *Black Jack*, or *Smith*, this book, one feels, should be in the adult section, because adults will be better equipped to get most value from it.

Leon Garfield's books, in fact, like those of some other writers, raise the question whether, in an age when the telling of straight narrative stories is no longer acceptable in adult novels, some writers may not be driven into children's books as the only way to make use of the gift that has been given them. I remember hearing an Australian writer, Ivan Southall, tell a seminar audience that this was why he wrote children's books, and one wonders whether Leon Garfield and perhaps also another borderline writer, Alan Garner, whose books will be considered later (p. 143), may not be novelists *manqués*.

Leon Garfield's work has been highly praised, and many good critics admire it, but it seems to me too early for a reliable judgement to be formed on it. His reputation is of very recent growth. His first book, *Jack Holborn*, was not published until 1964—too late for his work to be considered in John Rowe Townsend's book—and I know of no published study, though there have, of course, been many reviews in periodicals as the books came out. It is always difficult for an adult critic to be completely objective about children's books—so many of them are so much beneath notice to an informed mind that anything at all unusual stands out sometimes undeservedly—and this is particularly so with a writer like Leon Garfield who is, as he himself so shrewdly analysed, doing something that is neither quite for adults nor quite for children. But it seems unlikely that he can continue to produce at regular intervals a succession of the same kind of pseudo-historical firework displays. If he does, he will become type-styled and of less interest, but he has such obvious talent, as a born novelist of the true story-telling kind, that he may well develop his work along other lines that are of more interest to critics and readers like myself, to whom his present work does not greatly appeal because of its basic unreality.

There are other authors than Leon Garfield who have seen the need for books for new kinds of readers. Garfield's work has been considered here, partly because it is primarily adventure fiction (or of that kind) partly because he is rather a special case. More general books of this contemporary kind will be considered later, in the final section 'Novels for Young Readers'. Historical stories and fantasies, however, do still seem to be written, and read, as separate categories. Librarians tell me that it is still common for children to read 'nothing but fantasies' for long periods and that there are stages when children, girls in particular, like nothing better than historical stories. These two classifications have therefore been retained.

An oddity that might, however, as well be considered here as anywhere is science fiction. When stories of this kind first began to appear they were thought of as fantasy. They tended to be about strangely shaped (or constructed) beings and their authors used considerable imagination in the development of plots based largely on scientific and intellectual developments that seemed then beyond the range of thought. But fact caught up with fantasy fast and by the time that science fiction had spread from the adult field into children's fiction—which it did rather late in the day—space travel was becoming an accepted fact. Science fiction stories, as a result, have in the main ceased to be thought of as fantasy. Adult science fiction writing has tended to become moralistic, using new devices and new confrontations to present in seemingly new ways what are, in fact, the old familiar issues: science fiction for children has become just another kind of adventure story. Science fiction has, in fact, as yet made no significant contribution to children's literature. It seems unlikely that it will do so, because there is an artificiality about the whole topic that is unattractive to most writers. The probability is, therefore, that this will become another completely stereotyped category, consisting largely of what John Rowe Townsend has described as 'unedifying stories of interplanetary or instellar war'.

There was a time when it seemed that it might do better than that. As long ago as 1940 (before science fiction was seriously thought of as a category) Donald Suddaby wrote an imaginative story, *Lost Men in the Grass*, which is still at least as good as most stories with that now too familiar theme and deserves more recognition than it has received. Donald Suddaby is a much under-rated writer and his later books, *The Death of Metal*, *Star Raiders* and *Prisoners of Saturn*, would probably be more admired if they were published today than they were when they first appeared. But most stories of this kind have their origins in the pioneering imagination of H. G. Wells, whose *The War of the Worlds* and brilliant short stories are still as good as anything written in this field—and better than most—and can still be read with enjoyment by children lucky enough to be introduced to them, even though they may originally have been written for adults.

Historical Stories

In the last twenty years there has been a strong revival of interest in historical stories. Although there were many writers of 'historical novels for children' in the first half of the century, most of them were nearer to adventure stories than history and all were marred by an excess of a false type of dialogue that came to be known as 'gadzookery'. Their plots, too, were absurdly artificial, dragging in (and too often distorting) historical events by the scruffs of their necks, as it were, in order to include them, rather than incorporating them naturally and logically in the development of plot and character. As a result historical stories fell into disrepute, being regarded as a largely false form. What was needed was a writer of calibre to give them a new image.

In the first half of the century the only writer to attempt this was Geoffrey Trease, whose books have already been mentioned (p. 90). He made the first serious attempt to incorporate a proper treatment of history in books for children. To him, undoubtedly, must go the credit for setting a new style towards a more conscientious, properly researched story of the past that concerned itself as much with the social events of its time, and their effects on the people who lived in them, as with excitement and action. When new writers emerged it was this line, rather than the old Ballantyne, Henty and Herbert Strang one that they followed, and though none of Trease's books ever quite lived up to the promise of his ideas he must be acknowledged as a pioneer.

The first, and still the most outstanding of this new kind of historical writer for children was Rosemary Sutcliff. She has since been at least matched, in maturity and in her depth of knowledge of her chosen periods by other writers, and it is no longer as rare as it was when she first began writing to find warmth and sympathy, good dialogue and fine plots in historical stories for children. But she still stands head and shoulders above most of them. It is not easy to convey the power of her books. It is due to many things—passionate convictions convincingly communicated; a strong sense of history (real history, not just Kings and Queens, Knights in

Armour and Battles) and a fine, compelling style—but most of all to the fact that she is a born writer. This is the thing she needed to do, and she does it supremely well. It is difficult for me to write objectively of her work, for I read her first books in manuscript and still remember the pleasure with which we all read *The Queen Elizabeth Story* when it arrived on my desk, unexpectedly, at a time when she was supposed to be working on another commission. No one could have had any idea then of the books to come, for that is a simple tale, however charmingly told, but we all experienced that unmistakable feeling that one gets when one recognises the birth of a real writer. How rarely that happens!

Illustration by Charles Keeping for Dawn Wind, *by Rosemary Sutcliff (Oxford University Press).*

Margaret Meek, in her Bodley Head monograph on Rosemary Sutcliff's work, has given an account of her development that could hardly be bettered, and the best of her books are so well known that it would be pointless to attempt to analyse them here. The great ones, from *The Eagle of the Ninth* onwards, all give the reader an extraordinary sense of involvement, of being personally concerned with a deeply felt series of events and emotions that is being projected from inside rather than written about from the outside. The sequence of books about Roman Britain, in particular, *The Eagle of the Ninth*, *The Silver Branch* and *The Lantern Bearers*, paint an astonishingly vivid picture of the Britain of that time, which must have taught countless thousands of children more about history than all the textbooks—and is likely to continue doing so. *The Lantern Bearers* is notable for a remarkable set of illustrations that show Charles Keeping stretched to his best as a black and white artist—just as the reader will be stretched to appreciate the book to the full, which is as it should be.

A writer with the same convictions about history as Rosemary Sutcliff, who wrote a number of historical stories for children that are all worth reading, was Henry Treece. He wrote many books but only the best of them achieve any real stature. Too many of them have the air of a professional exercise, and his plots lack subtlety and skill, being, for all their basis on genuine research and true historical understanding, much nearer in their treatment of character and dialogue to the older tradition of historical novel. Comparison of *The Eagles Have Flown* or *The Legions of the Eagle* with *The Eagle of the Ninth* or *The Lantern Bearers* is illuminating.

High on any literate boy's list of best books will be the historical novels of Ronald Welch, for they are full of the kind of action which boys enjoy and contain enough detail about swords, guns and other weapons to delight any boy's heart. Often, when one of the family has wanted to know what a sword or gun described in some other book looks like, my son has said, 'I know where to find that!' It is sure to be in one or other of the Carey books, and he will know which one. This sort of intimate acquaintance with the whole of a writer's work is unusual with children's writers and it is a mark of Ronald Welch's success that he has so widely achieved it. His series of books about the Carey Family, beginning with *Knight Crusader*, a powerful book that won him the Carnegie Medal for 1954, and continuing with various members of the

Illustration by William Stobbs for Knight Crusader, *by Ronald Welch (Oxford University Press).*

family right up to the nineteenth century with *Nicholas Carey*, are very different from Rosemary Sutcliff's. They are more practical, more concerned with action—primarily military action—but their history is as true, even if it is nearer to the surface, and he must have given many boys a new under-standing of what all those battles in the history books were about.

Hester Burton, another outstanding historical writer, is nearer to Rosemary Sutcliff's approach to history, being more interested in how history affects people but her books lack the latter's warmth of feeling for period and character. They cover a wide spread of history, but all are concerned with the social conditions of their time, and the involvement of her characters in them. *Time of Trial*, which won her the Carnegie Medal for 1964, deals with social conditions in London at the beginning of the nineteenth century and the difficulties of a publisher who condemns them; *No Beat of Drum* deals with the effects of the Industrial Revolution on the agricultural workers of England in the nineteenth century and with trans-portation to Tasmania for minor offences; *Thomas*, a more recent book, is concerned with Quakers and religious persecution in the time of the Great Plague. It is a more complex book than her earlier ones and difficult reading even for older children, but a satisfying one.

Hester Burton has also written two stories about more recent times, *The Great Gale* and *In Spite of All Terror*, which are interesting experiments in realism. The first, based on the great floods in 1953 on the East Coast of England, is almost documentary in its severely factual treatment. The second is more fictional but still, in its descriptions of bombing raids on London and other war-time events, stays close to reality. Neither is outstanding, but they have their place in assessing her work as a whole.

Even more demanding for young readers are the novels of Stephanie Plowman. Her two books about Russia, *Three Lives for the Czar* and *My Kingdom for a Grave*, follow the story of the Hamilton family through the days of the last Czar to the Revolution in a style and treatment that make no concessions to young peoples' vocabularies or comprehensions. The tragic story is seen through the eyes of Andrei Hamilton, first as an idealistic boy only half understanding the events which darken the lives of his family and later as a still deeply committed but tragically disillusioned young officer. The style is dry, taut, cerebral and the author has wisely made no attempt to superimpose an artificially developed plot on the known historical events. There are none of the trappings of the traditional, or even the more recent, historical novel for children—even one by Rosemary Sutcliff. The incidents of history are dramatic, tragic and traumatic enough, but they are not centred on the narrator and neither his actions nor his character influence them in any way. Andrei suffers, indeed, but there is no real conflict and there is no triumph—even his suffering comes to the reader through so restrained, almost laconic a commentary that the reader's tears, if he sheds any, must be for humanity, not for Andrei.

These two fine books are so far removed from any previous historical writing for children that it is difficult to see them in perspective. As the anonymous reviewer of the first of them in *The Times Literary Supplement* said, in a finely perceptive assessment, they are 'no more children's novel[s] than *War and Peace* or *Dr Zhivago*', an illuminating comparison, for that is where they stand. These are simply fine novels, for whoever cares to read them—and infinitely better than most historical writing for adults. In any true assessment of them as books in their own right the question of whether or not they were written for children becomes irrelevant—as does the fact that *The Lord of the Rings* or *The Sword in the Stone* were originally written for adults. But their position in the general development of British writing for children *is* relevant to the purposes of this book and must therefore be assessed.

That adults admire them greatly is unquestionable. But how accessible are they to children? And what, if that question must be asked, do we mean nowadays by 'children'? Miss Plowman's publishers have inserted on the title pages of these two books the catch phrase *'Novels for New Adults'*. It is not, perhaps, a particularly happy term, but it is an honest one and it probably establishes fairly enough the level at which such books will be read. The style demands concentration. What would a professional children's editor even fifteen years ago have said to an author who began the third chapter of her book (with no previous reference to the characters referred to) with such a sentence as:

> 'But a far more exalted couple did not share my family's objective affection for Russia, even though, as my Grandfather remarked during his second visit to Russia in 1895, in view of Catherine II's morals it was hardly likely that the Czar was any more Russian by blood than father was.'?

The depth of compassion and understanding needed to appreciate the books fully is surely beyond the range of most young people.

Stephanie Plowman is a deeply committed writer, basing carefully thought-out documentary-type historical stories on long and scholarly research, but it is difficult to see her as a writer for children. It is not easy, in fact, to understand why it was necessary for these two novels ever to have been published as children's books. One would have thought that they would have succeeded equally as adult novels. But it may have been thought that since the books, lacking as they do any sustained romantic interest or adventure, are not likely to appeal to readers of the popular type of historical fiction for adults, they stood more chance of success with 'new adults'.

Cynthia Harnett, a schoolteacher, also treats history seriously in carefully detailed studies of life in England at different times: *Ring Out Bow Bells!*, *The Load of Unicorn*, *The Great House*, *Stars of Fortune*, and *The Wool-pack*. Her books, with her own drawings of tools, buildings and other

Illustration by William Stobbs from his book *The Three Little Pigs*
(The Bodley Head).

Illustration by Pauline Baynes for *A Dictionary of Chivalry* (Longman).

exact period detail looked fresh and unusual when they first appeared but now begin to have a somewhat old-fashioned appearance. They are still good solid books, full of information for those who genuinely want to learn, but their stories are not sufficiently compelling to attract today's young readers and her characters rarely come to life.

Better novelists, and almost equally good historians—though with less deliberate detail and more character in their stories—are Hilda Lewis and Barbara Leonie Picard. Hilda Lewis's *Harold Was My King* and *The Gentle Falcon* (a story of Richard II's child-queen Isabella) are two fine novels which make one wish she had written more for children. Barbara Leonie Picard has written only for children, in a number of different fields: some moving original fairy stories; a group of convincing retellings of old stories (the Odyssey, the Iliad, The Norse Mythology, the King Arthur Stories and collections of French and German legends, of which the Odyssey and King Arthur are the most impressive) and three historical novels. These, *One Is One*, *Lost John*, and *Ransom*

Drawing by Gareth Floyd for The Grove of Green Holly, *by Barbara Willard (Longman).*

for a Knight are all set in the Middle Ages and form an interesting link between the traditional historical novel and the contemporary version, for though the historical detail is accurate enough to satisfy historians they are much more concerned with the adventures and characters of their young heroes and heroines. She writes exceptionally well and her narratives flow with that seemingly effortless assurance that is so important for young readers in preventing any interruption in the suspension of disbelief.

It is difficult to do justice to the whole of contemporary work in this field without comment degenerating into listing. For there are many writers whose work twenty years ago would have seemed outstanding but now suffers from comparison by newer standards. Barbara Willard's gentle tales, for example, *The Grove of Green Holly*, *The Lark and the Laurel* and others, have a natural unstretching charm that appeals to many girls, and Madeleine Polland, Barbara Softly, Winifred Cawley and J. G. Fyson have all produced books that in a less demanding age would have seemed outstanding.

Fantasy

Although our writers are now creating fine works for children in a number of different fields—historical stories, stories of everyday adventure, stories of contemporary life, school stories—it remains true that most critics, if asked to name outstanding books, tend to think first of fantasies.

One of the reasons for this is, no doubt, the very practical one that it is harder to name a single outstanding book by relatively prolific writers like Rosemary Sutcliff or William Mayne than it is to name a single work of true imaginative invention like *Tom's Midnight Garden*, *The Children of Green Knowe* or *The Hobbit*. But it is also true that those who write historical or adventure stories, school stories or realistic novels tend to become regarded as professionals in their field. They produce a book a year or more, usually of much the same kind, and tend to become type-stamped. True fantasy is a much rarer thing, often the only book (or series of books) of its kind by a writer whose normal work is altogether different.

The threads drawing the British creative instinct to fantasy are strong and closely interwoven with that part of it which is responsible for its poetry. Helen Lourie[1] has drawn attention to the fact that so many of the greatest writers of fantasy have been men, and on reflection this does not surprise us—even though it may not be wholly valid. The truest fantasies are not only a high form of creation but are also closely allied to poetry and in this, as in music, women have rarely excelled —which makes it the more surprising that they should have done so well in fantasies for children.

Another reason why the truest fantasies are often isolated works is that they are the hardest to write. It is difficult to imagine a professional writer of fantasies, for the fire in the belly that warms a writer's imagination to create something that to him needed to be said and could be said best only in a fantasy, can rarely be rekindled after it has burnt itself out.

That something that needs to be said is usually a statement

[1] Helen Lourie, 'Where is Fancy bred', *New Society*, 6 December, 1962.

about man and his nature, and about the life we live on this earth, that is nearer to truth and tells us more about ourselves and what we need to know than much so-called realistic writing. We live in a complex and troubled society and those growing up into it, who will have to carry its burdens into the future, need help to be able to tell right from wrong, the true course from the wrong course, clearly and instinctively. They are unlikely to derive this early, instinctive faith from troubled and confused books which paint an only too real picture of the problems they will have to face, and blur rather than define the borderlines between true and false values. It is right that children should be given such books, when they are capable of understanding what can be learnt from them, but they need to get their values right first and this is the true importance of the better kind of fantasy.

The extraordinary growth of interest in folk tales and fairy tales, and in myths and legends of all kinds, during the past twenty years has already been mentioned. It is tempting to see such reading as a form of escape and that, no doubt, it partly is, but there is a deeper and more important motive for it. In reading myths, and the kinds of fantasy that is being discussed here, children are instinctively reaching towards the right solutions, just as did the first man who reached for a dock leaf when he stumbled into a bed of nettles. In *The Ordinary and the Fabulous* Elizabeth Cook has emphasised that 'Fabulous stories illuminate the ordinary world and if they also illuminate a "world to come" it is not like the world of daydreaming'. C. S. Lewis was making the same point when he said, 'The real victim of wishful reverie does not batten on *The Odyssey*, *The Tempest* or *The Worm Ouroboros*: he (or she) prefers stories about millionaires, irresistible beauties . . . things that might really happen, that ought to happen, that would have happened if the reader had had a fair chance. For there are two kinds of longing. The one is an *askesis*, a spiritual exercise, the other is a disease.'[1]

All this may seem far removed from those joyous stories which delight the very young, like Richard and Florence Atwater's *Mr Popper's Penguins*, Christianna Brand's *Nurse Matilda* or Barbara Sleigh's *Carbonel*. Often these, too, have their place, but it was not this sort of book that C. S. Lewis or Elizabeth Cook were talking about. For there are two kinds

[1] C. S. Lewis, 'On Three Ways of Writing for Children', *Proceedings of The Bournemouth Conference 1952*, The Library Association, London.

of fantasy. The first is a story about ordinary life but with some extra quality added—the power to have wishes granted, to travel into the past or the future, to talk to animals; or the introduction of creatures or people who do not belong to real life. The adventures that happen to the children in this kind of story—they nearly always involve quite young children—are fantastic enough, but the child has the constant reassurance that they are happening in the real world. The other kind of fantasy is either about a different world altogether, often about a completely different order of beings; or about our own world but in a completely different time, either the remote past or the unforeseeable future, in which everything is different. Strangely enough, this second kind, the one that seems superficially the further removed from real life, is usually nearer to its truth than the other kind.

These two kinds of fantasy are not always clearly distinguishable, nor is it easy to set a time at which children will be ready to read any sort of fantasy. So there is a constant overlap between both category and age of reading which makes classification difficult. Some of the books discussed in this section could well have been included in the section on 'The In-Between Books' (and vice versa) but have been included here for convenience in considering together a group of books of roughly the same kind.

The first kind of fantasy is the easiest to read, and the one which most children take to more naturally, because it is not so far removed from the subject matter of a great deal of their earliest reading. Some of these books have already been mentioned: *Winnie-the-Pooh*, *Mary Poppins*, *Mumfie*, *Paddington*, and their kind are the beginnings of fantasy and it is a very short step from *Mary Poppins*, via *Bedknob and Broomstick*, to *The Borrowers*.

Mary Norton's *The Borrowers*, first published in 1952, was a brilliant feat of imagination. Her conception of the little people who live under the floorboards on odds and ends borrowed from humans, is not only almost perfectly conceived to delight the mind of a small child, but it has the inspired logic of the best fantasies, for it seems to fit so well with the thoughts that even adults have about the mysterious way in which small things disappear. It had been preceded by another book about a Lilliputian world, *Mistress Masham's Repose* by T. H. White, a finely written novel about a girl's discovery of descendants of the Lilliputians living on an island in a private lake. But the two books are completely different and

Mistress Masham's Repose was originally an adult novel—
though a very odd one for adults—and will only be enjoyed
by older children.

Mary Norton wrote three other books about her family of
Borrowers, Pod, Homily and Arrietty: *The Borrowers Afield*,
The Borrowers Afloat and *The Borrowers Aloft* and, surprisingly, though the original book remains the best, she
contrived to sustain the reality, humour and brilliant inven-
tiveness of her story to the end. Of all the contemporary
fantasies for younger children *The Borrowers* is probably the
most successful—and enjoyable.

Completely different in approach and posing different problems to the young reader, because children who are able to
take the straightforward inventions of *The Borrowers* in their
stride are less happy in the deeper world of personal magic,
is the kind of story that is typified by Catherine Storr's
Marianne Dreams, in which Marianne, ill in bed, finds a
magic pencil and with it draws herself into the life of a sick
boy and in helping him to get well solves some of her own
problems. Catherine Storr's books are mainly of this kind.
Rufus is about a small, unhappy orphaned boy who steals a
knife from his teacher which magically transports him into
the past, where he learns to stand up for himself; and in *Robin*
another boy finds a magic shell with similar results.

In this group also belongs Joan G. Robinson's *When Marnie
Was There*. Once again an introspective and solitary child
finds companionship and strength in an elusive companionship, this time the teasing, delightful Marnie, seen first at
the window of a house that has been empty for many years.
This is a beautifully written, memorable book that is outstanding among contemporary fantasies.

Many children who felt themselves neglected, or simply
lonely and insecure, must have comforted themselves by
inventing imaginary companions. But children are, on the
whole, logical creatures, aware that there are complications
about human beings coming out of the blue. Animals, on the
other hand, often seem to a child's mind to do just that—
father brings home suddenly a cat, or a dog, or a bird—where
did it come from? Why should not just such a companion
appear suddenly for them? It is not surprising, therefore, that
a number of fantasies should have this theme. One of the best
of them is Anne Barrett's *Midway*, in which an older boy,
unsure of himself and plagued by the weakening fears and
doubts of adolescence, conjures up an imaginary tiger,

Midway, to be his companion and give him strength. Books like this sound unconvincing when badly described, but this is a remarkable book that deserves to be better known. Philippa Pearce's *A Dog So Small* is another book with this theme, but this will be considered later in a general discussion of her work. Finally, in this highly selective list, comes Clive King's *Stig of the Dump*. This time the small boy falls accidentally into a disused pit and invents (or does not invent but discovers—for this story has elements of time shift as well as compensatory fantasy) a prehistoric cave man, Stig, living in it. For a time he shares Stig's adventures and the two lives interweave, much as they do in Philippa Pearce's other fantasy, *Tom's Midnight Garden*—but with what a difference! Many children enjoy *Stig of the Dump* because it can be read at a second level as so many children do read, simply as an adventure, without thought of what the author's motives were. But it is not completely convincing as a fantasy.

All these books have been chosen as examples of one sort of fantasy. The imagined tale that is really a moral one; that is, in which the fantasy serves what is really a moral purpose —to convince children that they should be more understanding of others' difficulties; that they should be kinder to less fortunate children; that they need not suffer as they do from imaginary fears; that they are braver than they think they are—that their own lives are not so bad after all.

Another kind of fantasy is the gaily unreal adventure that uses magic purely for fun, such as Nicholas Stuart Gray's *Grimbold's Other World*, about a little boy and his magic cat; John Onslow's *The Stumpfs*, about the last good witches left in England, or Barbara Sleigh's *Carbonel*, a gaily natural tale about a little girl who buys a black cat from a retiring witch and has to go to a lot of trouble to free it from the witch's spell. There are many stories of this kind, for they are relatively easy to invent, and there is no point in cataloguing them all.

On the borderline between the youngest fantasies and those for older children come the works of two writers of an earlier period, Eleanor Farjeon and Patricia Lynch. Eleanor Farjeon came from a family of writers and was warmly involved in the literature of her time. She knew many writers and poets (the letters she exchanged with Edward Thomas have been published and she wrote discerningly about his work) and was widely known herself. In a long life associated with writing and publishing one meets a number of authors who are better known and admired for what they were than for what they wrote and Eleanor Farjeon would come high on any such list. She was an outgoing, warm-hearted, impulsive, completely genuine human being and no one who knew and loved her would ever want to write slightingly of her work. But it must be acknowledged that her substantial and, at the time, well-deserved reputation was established largely because she began writing at a time when, apart from Walter de la Mare, there was little else that was worth notice being written for children. At a time when there was little quality to be found she cared for quality, and as a writer of graceful verse and a born story-teller with a light sense of humour, she achieved many successes in a long and prolific career. The best of her genuine talent is found in her short stories, such as *Jim at the Corner* and the two *Martin Pippin* books, and this was acknowledged by the award to her, towards the end of her writing career, of the Carnegie Medal in 1955 and the first International Hans Christian Andersen Award in 1956, both for another collection of stories, *The Little Bookroom*. But though she was a much-loved writer she wrote little at full length, and despite a remarkable second flowering of her work after its re-discovery by Oxford University Press, it seems unlikely that it will endure, because it belongs essentially to an age and an era of writing for children that is now past.

Patricia Lynch's tales of the Irish countryside are of that special kind in which magic and the everyday are inextricably interwoven. In *The Turf Cutter's Donkey* leprechauns move about freely, animals talk, anything and everything is likely to become enchanted at any moment and to resume its natural form as easily, and this same gift is revealed in *The Grey Goose of Kilnevin* and other books. Her stories have a seeming casualness and lightness that is deceptive, for there is more truth, and more carefully detailed observation of real life, in them than appears on the surface. The human figures in her stories are always well drawn, natural and normal to the scenes in which the stories are set, and the tales themselves derive genuinely from folk-lore. This sort of earthy, folk-lorish naturalness seems to sit most easily on regional writers, for it is found in perhaps even stronger form in Mollie Hunter's books about Highland crofters and kelpies. *The Kelpie's Pearls*, a story about the boy who, because he had the 'King Solomon's Ring' gift of being able to attract animals, came to be regarded as a witch's familiar, is one of the clearest-hearted and most attractive contemporary stories of its kind.

As has been mentioned earlier there has been a remarkable revival of interest, in recent years, in books about witches. There are witches, serious or humorous, in fantasies of many kinds. But there is also a surprising number of well-written and convincing books, usually for girls, which contain sustained and sometimes frightening treatments of the witchcraft theme. One of the best of these is *Moon Eyes* by Josephine Poole, a menacing little tale about a familiar in the form of a black dog, and an evil aunt with designs on a little boy. The boy is saved by the other child in the story, a young girl, and their two characters are well drawn, with much carefully observed and lovingly described detail. This is a very real book, which must leave many children with a conviction that witches *could* exist. As must also Ruth M. Arthur's *A Candle in her Room,* a more ambitious book that describes the effect on three generations of girls of a thoroughly nasty little wooden doll with evil powers. This is a real story about real people that if put in the adult section of a library could be read by adults without question. There are so many other stories for girls about witches or witchcraft that there must be some special attraction for them in this theme—but that is probably a study for the psychologist rather than the critic.

Drawing by Robin Jacques for The Sea Piper, *by Helen Cresswell (Chatto, Boyd and Oliver).*

Finally, before coming to the major fantasies of the period (which defy classification) there is a group of stories which, although in many respects widely different, all use the device of setting a seemingly naturalistic tale in a period which either never existed or was not as described. The first of these were Helen Cresswell's beguilingly dead-pan tall-tales. These are, to some readers, an acquired taste and not all children enjoy them. But to those fortunate few who are capable of the complete suspension of disbelief that is necessary to appreciate them fully they are enchanting. In this world or another world (it doesn't really matter) and in an unidentifiable time, a group of completely convincing people live out an adventure or an episode, which is either madly absurd or completely logical according to the way the reader sees it. In *The Pie-makers*, Arthy and Jem Roller have been hereditary piemakers for generations in a village called Danby Dale. In the nearby village of Gorby Dale lives Crispin Roller, Arthy's brother and rival piemaker, and the story concerns nothing more (or less) than the rivalry between the two families over the making of a giant pie for the King. The pie is so vast that it takes twenty men to haul it from the shed in which it was made. It is a wonderful pie—how many children must have dreamt of just such a pie! But—'I think perhaps it could have done with just a shade more parsley' observes one of the characters at the end of the book and that is a not uncommon reaction. Like *Stig of the Dump*, the book needs to be swallowed whole and if the reader can't do that he misses most of the flavour.

Joan Aiken's imaginative short stories have already been mentioned. Her full-length books are mostly lighthearted unrealities which describe the riotous adventures of spirited, good-hearted children and outrageously overdrawn adults in a period of English history that never happened—the Stuarts, in the person of good King James III, are on the throne in the nineteenth century, and the forests are full of wolves. Her first book, *The Wolves of Willoughby Chase*, is an enchantingly funny tale that is at once a riotous fantasy that almost becomes momentarily believable, so well is the story told, and a parody on all fantasies, Victorian melodramas, and any such other stories that ring false. Its sequel, *Black Hearts in Battersea*, is even funnier, and even more exciting. Absurd people and even absurder events crowd on each other thick and fast; there are shipwrecks, a balloon, more wolves and a glorious set piece that would make a fine dénouement for a marvellously funny film. *Night Birds of Nantucket* introduces a change of scene but not of manner and is equally enjoyable. A rather different kind of book, *The Whispering Mountain*, is more serious and, on the whole, less successful. Joan Aiken's books have sometimes been described as being funnier to adults than they are to children, and this may be true, but there is plenty of evidence that children enjoy them to the full and take the improbabilities in their stride.

In a somewhat similar vein are Rosemary Harris's two inventions of Ancient Egypt, *The Moon in the Cloud* and *The Shadow on the Sun*. Both Joan Aiken and Rosemary Harris also write adult suspense or detective stories—as does Peter Dickinson, the final writer in this group—and it is interesting that three authors of such stories should, when they turn to writing for children, all choose to set their stories in imaginary worlds. Rosemary Harris's Ancient Egypt has, in fact, much in common with Joan Aiken's wolves. It never happened, there is plenty of action, and it is very funny. But it is more consciously contrived and there are occasional false notes, of a kind of which Joan Aiken is not guilty—because she is more obviously simply having fun. The first book, *The Moon in the Cloud*, is set in the time of the flood. As the story begins Noah is told by a somewhat disgruntled Lord God to get busy on the Ark. Nearby is camped an itinerant animal trainer, Reuben, with his wife, Thamar. Noah refuses them room in the Ark but his son Ham who is, for the purpose of the story, a dissolute scoundrel, strikes a bargain with Reuben. If Reuben will make the dangerous journey south into Kemi (Egypt) and bring back the two great cats that Noah has told Ham to find, he, Ham, will somehow get Reuben and his wife onto the Ark. Reuben undertakes the task and makes the journey south with his three animal friends, the camel, Anak, the herd dog, Benoni, and the cat, Cefalu. They are all captured by the cruel High Priest of Sekhmet and Reuben becomes the slave of the young King. After many adventures they all finally escape and are reunited with Thamar, who has come part of the way to find them (and escape from Ham's attentions). Ham is accidentally killed while goading one of Reuben's elephants; the Lord God graciously allows Reuben to become a substitute for Ham and board the Ark with his wife and when you read about Ham in the Bible it was Reuben all the time . . .

That is one of the touches which rings a slightly false note. An even sharper one is sounded when we are told that the

High Priest has a rhyme to help him remember the names of the Gods, which is only funny if you know *The Sound of Music*:

> 'Nut—a cow, a sacred cow
> Re—a god of golden sun'

and so on, and is an unnecessarily easy jest in so gaily told and elegantly contrived an adventure. The second book, *The Shadow on the Sun*, continues Reuben's adventures after the Flood. The Flood was not a success—'only a man would have thought it would be' says Thamar. Noah is more drunken than ever and Shem and Japhet are beginning to regret Ham. Reuben has always wanted to return to Kemi and see the King again and he persuades Thamar and the animals to accompany him on a new journey. The King is in love with a beautiful young girl, who is captured by the savage Prince of Punt and put in the power of an evil sorceress M'bu. Reuben rescues her and everyone lives happily ever after. This is a less sophisticated book than *The Moon in the Cloud*, much more of a straight adventure-with-fantastic-trimmings and on the whole a disappointment, though it retains sufficient pace to be enjoyable.

The most interesting member of this group is Peter Dickinson, a comparatively new writer whose stories about 'The Changes', a time when men in England had learned to fear and dread machines, and so destroy them, have been one of the most refreshing discoveries of the last few years. His three books on this theme were not written chronologically. The first to be published, *The Weathermonger*, describes events long after the Changes and tells how its effects were finally reversed. The second, *Heartsease*, is about a middle period, with the Changes established as a normal part of everyday life, and not until the third book, *The Devil's Children*, is the time immediately following the Changes described.

The first of these three books, *The Weathermonger*, is a straightforward and vividly exciting adventure story. The Changes have only affected Britain; Europe is still as she was, but she cannot mount a rescue expedition because, for reasons which are described with convincing ingenuity, all forms of power fail as the English coast is approached. Two children are found who have been unaffected by the Changes. They are taken to France, given careful instructions and then taken across the Channel in a sailing yacht back to England. The expedition has been carefully planned, with the help of people from England who happened to be abroad at the time of the Changes and were thus unaffected, and the children make their landing at Beaulieu Abbey, where the motor museum is known to have been left untouched. Lord Beaulieu, who was in France, has given them the keys to the Museum and to the famous Rolls-Royce, the Silver Ghost, which they have been told to take as the fastest and most reliable vehicle there. Their object is to drive across England to Wales, and get as near as they can to a spot which has been located as the source of the trouble. They succeed in doing this, discover the cause of the Changes and are able to reverse them. This is a wonderfully imaginative adventure story, of a kind that seemed almost to have ceased to exist, and no one who has read it will be surprised that its author should also have written a series of detective stories (or something like detective stories) which are as unique in their own way as *The Weathermonger* is among children's adventure stories of today. The second book about The Changes, *Heartsease*, is even better, because the story is just as exciting but there are also strongly drawn characters. The girl who is the centre of the story is clearly drawn and the villagers and other adults are only too true to life. This is a story of prejudice and oppression, that paints an all-too-recognisable picture of what English villages could become in a time of such Change. Peter Dickinson's third book, *The Devil's Children*, takes the reader back to the beginning of the Changes. Nicky (another impressively realised girl) has been left alone in London to fend for herself. She joins a community of Sikhs who are escaping from the city to find a place in the country to settle. They adopt her as their 'canary', because their alien culture makes them impervious to the Changes, and only she can warn them of dangers. She learns to share their life, and after many difficulties becomes a valued member of the community. This is a book which, once the basic situation is accepted, is completely real. There are no gratuitous sensations, no thrills for the sake of thrills, and no easy solutions, but the author leaves us a believable hope.

The remaining fantasies in this group can only be considered individually, for they defy classification. An unusual story by Pauline Clarke, *The Twelve and the Genii*, was awarded the Carnegie Medal in 1962, the judges being partly influenced, one suspects, by the 'literary' element in its theme. A small boy, Max, finds the twelve toy soldiers with which the Brontës played as children. The stories which the Brontës invented as they played with these soldiers are, of course, known and these are re-enacted by the soldiers for Max and the reader. Though the plot sounds superficial, even meretricious, when summarised baldly like this, the book is very well done and holds attention while it is being read. But its 'other plane' aspects are not completely convincingly handled and there are aspects of it that are teasing and even exasperating to an adult reader. The soldiers themselves, for example: the author says that they are in a museum, but this is apparently not so; and, if they are lost and Max could not possibly have seen them anywhere (nor has he read about them or the adventures the Brontës played out with them) why should the soldiers and their stories suddenly come alive for this particular small boy? This is a tedious response, admittedly, but the fact that it is provoked by the book is a legitimate comment. Children at the right age can, of course, read the book as a straight adventure, without any such teasing doubts, simply as a story about a small boy who finds some soldiers who behave in what seems to children a natural enough way for toy soldiers. But if that is the author's intention the introduction of the Brontës seems unnecessary.

No such doubts are ever likely to trouble L. M. Boston's readers, for *her* fantasies are completely convincing. *The Children of Green Knowe* is one of the two, or perhaps three, best fantasies (and children's books) of the past twenty years. Green Knowe is the ancient house that is the centre of nearly all L. M. Boston's stories. It is a real house, genuinely ancient—it is reputed to be one of the oldest, if not the oldest private house still inhabited in England—and the life of the centuries that has enriched the stones of the old house by the river breathes magically into all the Green Knowe stories.

In the first Green Knowe book, *The Children of Green Knowe*, the boy Tolly who figures in several of them comes to the house to visit his grandmother, Mrs Oldknow. She is the sort of grandmother that every boy dreams of having; kind but not fussy; helpful but not interfering; sympathetic when necessary, but most of the time just pleasantly but not obtrusively around when needed, as a sort of benevolent spirit. Mrs Oldknow tells Tolly, during this first holiday, the story of Green Knowe's history and as she talks her tales come to life in his mind and he and the reader move backwards and forwards in time. Gradually the children of the past, Linnet, Toby and Alexander (who had all died together tragically in the Great Plague) come to life for Tolly and fill the house enchantingly and most movingly with their presences and he finds himself back in time re-living their adventures. It is a fine flight of imagination, beautifully conceived and superbly executed, quite beyond criticism, and it is difficult for anyone at all sensitive to atmosphere to read it unmoved. This is one of the rare books written for children which reverses the normal process—by which adult books come to be read by children. This is a children's book that can be read, enjoyed and admired equally, perhaps even more, by adults.

Each of L. M. Boston's books about Green Knowe has a charm of its own. *The Chimneys of Green Knowe* is another time-shift story; *An Enemy at Green Knowe* is a frighteningly real story about one of the most shockingly believable witches in children's fiction; and her Carnegie Medal winner, *A Stranger at Green Knowe*, is a completely different kind of story, about a giant gorilla, escaped from a zoo, who finds a temporary sanctuary in the wilder parts of the Green Knowe garden and is befriended by a small visitor. This is one of the most remarkable of Mrs Boston's books, and perhaps hardly counts as a fantasy. The last, so far, of the Green Knowe books, *The River at Green Knowe*, is a puzzling sort of book that seems not quite to succeed by the standards set by the other books, but would be remarkable from any other writer.

Although the same children appear in several of L. M. Boston's books they are not sequels in the accepted sense, nor do the books suffer from any of the sense of strain which is too often apparent when an author is striving to spin too much from the one thread. Each book obviously has its roots in something that has stirred her passions or her sympathies. *A Stranger at Green Knowe* was prompted by a photograph of a gorilla in the Zoo that she saw in *The Times*, and the perceptive reader will become aware of strongly held convictions about all manner of things: 'displaced' children, segregated blind children in homes, wild animals taken from their natural habitat, conventional ideas about right and wrong, religion and morality and, above all, art and music. Her house is an abiding passion and one imagines her brooding in her beautiful, wild garden, seeking ways to weld the latest preoccupation into a story about Green Knowe and its garden. Each book takes a long time, for she would be dissatisfied with anything but a perfect grafting of the bud onto the stem and she has in consequence not written many books, for she is above all an artist. She writes clearly, simply and well, in a controlled, spare style that neither intrudes nor fails to communicate anything that she wants her readers either to understand or to feel, and her characters always come completely alive and appear to think and feel, and be affected by atmosphere and events, exactly as one feels such people should. Her work, to my mind, almost completely disproves Helen Lourie's remark about the best fantasies being written by men, because *The Children of Green Knowe* is one of the loveliest fantasies ever written, and it could not conceivably have been written by a man.

Any more than could the other perfect fantasy of our time, Philippa Pearce's *Tom's Midnight Garden*. This deeply moving, beautifully written and completely convincing time-fantasy is one of the most perfectly conceived and executed children's books of the past twenty years. It is a measure of its strength, and of the power it has to enthrall even adult readers, that John Rowe Townsend, a staunch advocate of realism, should say of it, a fantasy, that 'if I were asked to name a single masterpiece of English children's literature since the last war . . . it would be this outstandingly beautiful and absorbing book'.[1]

It is difficult to describe the plots of such books without spoiling them for the reader, for one is always conscious of the poet's caution, 'tread softly, for you tread on my dreams.' Tom is sent away to spend the holidays with his uncle and aunt. They live in an old house which has been converted into flats by its original owner, old Mrs Bartholomew, who still lives upstairs in one of the flats. There is nowhere to play, even the garden at the back has been sold and built upon, and there is only a small ugly yard. In the hall, which is the only unconverted part of the original house, stands a grandfather clock. It has never been moved because the screws holding it to the wall have rusted in, and it is the chiming of this clock, with some help from his aunt's too-rich cooking (which keeps him awake) that first draws Tom back into the past. He steals downstairs, opens a back door which he had not previously noticed—and finds himself in the lovely garden of the old house. At first he thinks that his uncle and aunt have been cheating him by pretending that there was no garden, but when he finds the real back door next morning and discovers that the garden has gone he realises that he was dreaming. Or he thinks he was, but the next night he goes downstairs

---

[1] John Rowe Townsend, *Written for Children*, Garnet Miller, 1965.

Illustration by John Burningham for his book *Borka, The Adventures of a Goose With No Feathers* (Jonathan Cape).

Illustration by Helen Oxenbury for *The Great Big Enormous Turnip*, by
Alexei Tolstoy (Heinemann).

again and the garden is still there, only it is subtly different. Over many nights he visits the garden, and gradually he realises that the days for him are years in the garden; that its seasons change in its own time, not his, and that the people he meets in it are living their own lives, unaware of his visitations, and growing old with the years that to him are nights. There are several children of the family in the garden and suddenly one night he realises that the little girl, Hatty, can see him, though none of the other children can. The other children do not treat her kindly, and she is grateful for his companionship. He and Hatty play together; he visits her in her bedroom when she is ill, and through her he becomes aware that time in the garden is not even moving constantly in one plane but that sometimes the children are younger,

Drawing by Susan Einzig for Tom's Midnight Garden, *by Philippa Pearce (Oxford University Press).*

sometimes older. The author makes beautifully subtle and complex use of this time-shift, and slowly the reader becomes aware that other influences than Tom's own dreaming are affecting what he sees. The time comes when Tom has to return home. Heartbroken at the thought of having to leave his garden he goes down again on the last night—and the garden has gone. Behind the door is only the yard, and there are no trees, no lawns—and no Hatty. Despairingly, from a full heart, he cries out her name and his uncle and aunt wake and hustle him to bed. In the morning old Mrs Bartholomew asks to see him, and he learns that she is Hatty. She has never forgotten him; they compare memories and exchange stories and he learns that she saw him in the garden many more times than he saw her—for he, in *her* childhood, was the imaginary boy she invented to keep her company in her loneliness as an unwanted and unloved orphaned relative. During the weeks that Tom has lived in the house she has been dreaming of the past. Tom realises that he has simply been a part of her dreams and discovers that the reason why the garden was not there the previous night was because that night she had been dreaming about her wedding—the first night for a long time she had not thought of him.

Such a story in other hands could be mawkish and unconvincing, just another time fantasy. In Philippa Pearce's it becomes almost unbearably moving. A wonderful book, one which children *can* read and enjoy, and many do, but which, as Lesley Aers said finely in a study of the treatment of time in children's books, 'is in many ways hardly a children's book at all; it is a cry from an adult awareness'.[1]

Although Philippa Pearce is generally accepted as one of the most important writers for children of the period, she has written comparatively little. She has never become a professional children's author—in the sense of writing regular, type-styled books, year after year—and her few books are all completely different. Her first connection with children's books seems to have been when she worked as an editor for Oxford University Press. During that time she wrote her first book, *Minnow on the Say*, and it is interesting to speculate that this book, which contains so many of the standard ingredients of successful children's stories, may well have been prompted by the feeling (all too common among editors!)

[1] Lesley Aers, 'The Treatment of Time in Children's Books', *Children's Literature in Education*, Vol. No. 2, Ward, Lock, 1970.

that she could do the same thing better. But this time the editor was right. She could. The 'Minnow' is a canoe, and its loss and rescue bring together two boys, David and Adam, from different family backgrounds. Although it is typical of the author's highly individual outlook that the social problem should be turned upside down and it is the bus driver's family that leads the happy, secure and well-fed life, while the upper class family is in difficulties, this is not a 'social consciousness' novel. It is a straightforward adventure story, with a long-sustained search for buried treasure by the river; a moderately nasty villain, an old mill, lovable (and unlovable) country characters, and even a happy ending. But the author's style and manner transmute these ordinary ingredients into pure gold and this is a fine book which, although not a fantasy, is unmistakably by the author who was shortly to produce *Tom's Midnight Garden*. To have been runner-up for the Carnegie Medal with one's first book and win it with one's second must be a rare feat, but Philippa Pearce achieved it, and deserved to. Her third book, *A Dog So Small*, proved to be completely unlike either *Minnow on the Say* or *Tom's Midnight Garden*. So much so that her first publisher apparently rejected it. It is an 'other dimension' fantasy, of the same general type as those which have already been described—in which a lonely, unhappy, or neglected child invents an imaginary companion. *Tom's Midnight Garden* is at least partly of this kind, but in that book the need is not really the centre of the story. In *A Dog So Small* it is, and this makes it nearer in kind to *Marianne Dreams* or *Midway*, though the treatment is quite different. A small boy passionately wants to have a dog of his own. He is not an unhappy boy, or one with any special problems; no one is unkind or unfeeling to him, and he is not hungry, or lonely, or sick, or in any genuine way deprived. He just wants a dog. From this small theme Philippa Pearce has created an unusual story. The boy creates in his own mind a minute dog, the smallest dog he can possibly think of. Later he identifies it as a Chihuahua and it becomes his constant companion. Thus far predictably. The twist in the tale, that makes it different from the other stories of this kind, is that the boy becomes so attached to the dream dog that when he is at last given a real dog he is disappointed and doesn't like it, because he preferred the Chihuahua. But reality wins in the end.

Although Philippa Pearce has written several smaller books her only other full-length book is *The Children of the House*.

This is an adaptation for children of a book originally written for adults by Major Sir Brian Fairfax-Lucy. It is, as might be expected, well done, but it is a surprising thing for so original and creative a writer to have done. It will be interesting to see what she does next. Whatever it is, it will be original, imaginative, and written with truth and sincerity, for she creates a real world that is far removed from the imaginary worlds in which so many children's books are set.

Last of all comes a group of major fantasies; allegories, or parables that are likely to be high among this century's most important contributions to children's literature. T. H. White's *The Sword in the Stone* is the first of the epic tales that combine to tell the story of King Arthur: *The Once and Future King*. It is a brilliantly witty and richly imaginative account of the formative boyhood of the boy Wart, whose real identity many readers will not guess (unless they are told) until towards the end of the book, when he plucks the sword from the stone. It was not originally written for children, but most of them will enjoy it, and go on as they mature to *The Witch in the Wood*, *The Ill-Made Knight* and *The Candle in the Wind*. *The Sword in the Stone*, like all the greatest fantasies, can be read at several different levels and has more to offer at each of them. I have known it read successfully to children as young as six and nine, as simply a gay story about the improbable adventures of a boy growing up to be a knight—with most of the features which make such stories fun for young children: fantastic adventures, transformations, magic, and funny characters. It is doubtful, in fact, whether it is any longer an adult book; other than in the sense that *Robinson Crusoe*, *Gulliver's Travels*, and *Don Quixote* are of course still adults' books, even though it is as children that we first become acquainted with them.

C. S. Lewis's 'Narnia' books, beginning, for most children, with *The Lion, the Witch and the Wardrobe*, although *The Magician's Nephew* is the first in Narnian time, are the most widely read and enjoyed of all the contemporary 'other-world' fantasies. This sustained allegory is unlike most such series in that each book has something new and different to offer and there is no weakening of either inspiration or interest. After *The Lion, the Witch and the Wardrobe* come *Prince Caspian*, *The Voyage of the Dawn Treader*, *The Silver Chair*, *The Horse and His Boy*, and *The Last Battle*. As every parent who has had the pleasure of reading these aloud to his family will know, every child can find something to his own

Drawing by Pauline Baynes for The Lion, the Witch and
the Wardrobe, *by C. S. Lewis (Bles).*

taste, and pleasure, in one or other of them. For the Narnia tales are, in the very best sense of the word, children's books. They were conceived for children and designed, with great understanding and skill, to appeal to children, in order to say exactly what the author wanted to say—to children. It is ironical, and a curious reflection on the odd state into which the study of children's reading is bringing us, that they should nowadays frequently be criticised for what is, in fact, their strength. It must be admitted that, to adults, the Christian symbolism comes in too easy a guise and that for many of us dear old Aslan becomes rather a bore. But the books were not written for *us*, they were written for children and as stories for children they succeed wonderfully. It will be a sad day if the time ever comes when every book for children has to be intelligent enough to seem admirable in every respect to adult critics.

One book that would triumphantly survive such a test is *The Lord of the Rings*. Professor Tolkien's epic of Middle Earth was begun before the war, in *The Hobbit*. During and after the war he continued the story, which he used to send in letters to his son, and finally, having polished it to his own satisfaction, published it as a trilogy from 1954 to 1955, a volume at a time, impatiently awaited by a growing audience.

The Lord of the Rings was initially conceived as an adult book and its first success, amounting almost to that of a best-seller, came from sales to adults. But children did not take long to find it and now it is read as much by young people as by adults. There is, in fact, something of a movement against it by some adults, especially intellectuals, and there are almost as many people who profess to despise it as there are those who think it one of this century's lasting contributions to that borderland of literature between youth and age. There are few such books—*Gulliver's Travels*, *The Pilgrim's Progress*, *Robinson Crusoe*, *Don Quixote*, *Alice in Wonderland*, *The Wind in the Willows*—what else? For a book to reach in the first place a sufficient universality of appeal to achieve a wide distribution among readers of all kinds, and then to be able to sustain this through successive generations of children and adults calls for rare qualities. It must have a theme that is understandable, and acceptable, at all levels; it must be compellingly written, in such a way as to hold the reader's attention from first to last; above all, it must appeal to some deep-seated instinct in man, associated with his sense of right and wrong and social justice; his struggle to survive; his delight in the uncontaminated aspects of the world he has inherited. *The Lord of the Rings* is one of the few contemporary works to achieve all these and seems destined to become this century's contribution to that select list of books which continue through the ages to be read by children and adults with almost equal pleasure.

Like all books of its rare kind it can be read at many different levels. It can be read aloud to the very young (from seven onwards) as a marvellous adventure story. It serves a most valuable purpose, when read by older children, as an introduction to mythology. There has been, in the recent past, a distrust of mythology and teachers have found, especially in the United States, that *The Lord of the Rings* serves as a marvellous introduction. Children read it, are engulfed in it—and what an unforgettable experience it must be to read this when the world is still young—and from it reach forward to other, older and, some might say, more genuine stories of the same kind. But though the mythology of *The Lord of the Rings* is an invented one it is as true to the essential nature of all mythology as any other system. That is the author's great achievement.

The theme, like that of most epics, is basically a simple one, that of the Quest carried through against the forces of darkness and evil to its triumphant conclusion. Professor Tolkien has read widely and deeply in Early English and other sources and the mythologies of the world are subtly woven into his story. The High Elves are Celtic, the dwarfs and dragons Germanic; the Riders of Rohan are Old English (the influence of Beowulf is strong) and other elements, such as the seeming death and renewal of Gandalf, can be found in *The Golden Bough*. But this weight of learning is carried lightly and the average reader need never become aware of it—other than through the strength and conviction that this basis of scholarship and understanding adds to the story. For what has been built from enduring materials, of known universal appeal, is likely to inherit something of their power.

To this marvellously woven background of mythology Tolkien has added his own equally great creations. The Hobbits, as most readers will soon become aware, are simply people, but it has fulfilled the author's purpose finely to say what he wanted to say about the basic earthliness and commonsense of that side of the English character which he seems most to admire, through the medium of the Hobbits, who are not dwarfs but are not quite men either—though they

are capable of rising to heights of generosity and self-sacrifice
and their will to survive is indomitable. The Ents are another
fine conception and, as W. D. Emrys Evans has shown in a
paper on *The Lord of the Rings*, which is the best exposition
of it I have seen,[1] they represent a concentration of the feeling
that Tolkien obviously has for trees, as a symbol of the power
of green and growing things opposed to the modern mind of
metal and wheels represented by Saruman.

But the greatest of his creations is Gollum, the unhappy
half-man, half-four-footed amphibious creature, who is aptly
described by Sam Gamgee as 'always either Slinker or
Stinker'. Gollum represents the worse side of man's nature,
just as Frodo, the Ring Bearer, represents the better side, and
both are influenced constantly for good or evil by the power
of the Ring. In the end Frodo himself momentarily succumbs
and it is the over-reaching greed of Gollum which finally
destroys the Ring. Gollum, with his ever-pervading air of
darkness and slime and dissolution, his memorable conversa-
tions with himself about his 'precious', is an unforgettable
creation. Only an insensitive reader will fail to share something of his burden and come, in the end, almost to sympathise with this unhappy, only partly evil creature who is,
after all, but ourselves gone wrong and who could so easily—
at the moment in the night when he seeks to comfort the
exhausted Frodo but is repulsed by Sam—have been saved
from himself.

The contemporary adult criticism of *The Lord of the Rings*
is understandable. A reaction against any too sudden and too
great a success of this kind is to be expected; especially when,
against all expectation, a book of this kind becomes an adult
succès d'estime. Inevitably, many adults who have admired it,
particularly those with any lack of confidence in their own
standards of judgement, are later irritated with themselves
for having been 'taken in' by a children's book, as they now
see it, and express their exasperation with themselves in
criticism of the book. This communicates to other adults who
have not read it and the chain reaction sets in. But none of this
will have any effect on future readers, for the book itself is
secure, established firmly beyond challenge. The age at which
it will be read matters not in the slightest. W. D. Emrys
Evans thinks 'sixth-formers and undergraduates'; an Ameri-

[1] W. D. Emrys Evans, 'The Lord of the Rings', *The School
Librarian*, Vol. 16, No. 3, 1968.

can teacher thinks it should be used as a substitute for Greek mythology. My own children, and I know many others with the same experience, had it read aloud to them—all the way through, over months of nights—when they were eight and ten respectively and it became an inescapable demand. They have since twice read it through themselves, and I do not believe that they are especially unusual readers. The book, like all masterpieces of its kind, is enjoyable at almost any age, to anyone who is prepared to read it.

Novels for Young Readers

One of the toughest problems facing any critic of contemporary fiction for children is the fact that it is impossible, in any logical arrangement of the material, to do a number of things that are eminently desirable. It is obviously desirable, for example, to assess in one place the whole output of an important author—but ideally it should also be possible to assess in a single section the whole range of books of a single kind (school stories, historical stories, fantasy and so on) by all authors. It is equally desirable to be able to compare in a single section the work of the most outstanding authors—but their work covers not only different genres, but also widely different age levels.

There is no single solution to this problem. Writers for children appear to be much more catholic—or less consistent—in their choice of topics, and the audiences whom they address, than those who write for adults and though the work of some major authors can be conveniently dealt with in a single category—Rosemary Sutcliff and Stephanie Plowman in 'Historical Stories' or L. M. Boston and Philippa Pearce in 'Fantasy' for example—there are others whose work ranges from stories for the very young right up to novels which only the most intelligent and sophisticated adolescent will fully appreciate.

In this final chapter, therefore, although its concluding purpose is to consider some aspects of contemporary realistic writing for older children, the whole of the work of two major writers has also been considered. Alan Garner's work fits logically enough in this section—though Garner has also written for younger children—but William Mayne bestrides all sections and his work could equally logically have been included in 'School Stories', or 'Fantasy', some of it even in 'The In-Between Books', and all of it, defensibly, in 'Stories of Adventure'.

William Mayne's name must inevitably appear frequently in any discussion of the late twentieth-century children's book. Not only because, despite conflicting views about his work, all critics agree that it is important, but also because he has written so many different kinds of book, for so many different ages. He is the one living writer of real stature who has already established a secure reputation. Whatever else he may write from now on he has written sufficient to demonstrate an instinctive understanding of the real nature of children, an infallibly sure ear for the truth of children's conversation, and a subtly complex way of looking at life, people and things which makes him unique among contemporary writers.

There are still many people who argue about William Mayne's work, who say that children don't like his books; that they sit on the library shelves; above all, that children don't *talk* like that. Anyone who believes this has never listened properly to children talking among themselves. Few children may use the actual words or constructions that Mayne uses, but what he achieves, for those with ears to hear, is the authentic sound and *feel* of children talking.

William Mayne's use of dialogue is, in fact, the distinguishing mark of his work. Children (and adults) who do not enjoy the finely strung tension and wit of the kind of dialogue that he writes (and it *is* a sophisticated taste) are not likely to appreciate his books. Because, to a much greater extent than with any other contemporary writer for children, his stories are introduced, developed and concluded with talk. Not to such an extent that, as with Ivy Compton-Burnett's novels, if you do not concentrate on every single world of the dialogue you are likely to miss an essential part of the plot, but at least to the extent that if you have the kind of visual rather than intellectual imagination that demands constant description to keep you 'on scene' you are likely to miss the essential point of his books—and may even lose your way in them. There are few descriptive passages; he rarely sets a scene—and when he does it is not particularly well done—so that the reader sometimes has to work hard to understand what is being described. Instead the reader is made aware of the effect the scene had on the people who were present and becomes vividly aware of what it felt like to be there. His books are about people and feelings rather than things. A 'thing' is often the superficial centre of the plot (an old barge, a disused railway line, a boat, a 'parcel of trees') but it is the people who matter and what they are like is communicated to the reader not by description but by what they say. If he wants his readers to know that a boy who has just come into the room is big and burly and angry he rarely tells you that he is—instead, he makes him *sound* big and burly and angry.

William Mayne is particularly good at conveying by small details of dialogue the inevitable tensions of close family relationships, and there are many fine examples of this in his books. The beautifully poised relationship between Ainsley and his sister Alice in *Sand* is never explicitly stated—any more than Alice (even what she wears) is ever described, but we become aware of it from the first words we hear her speak. The nicely controlled, never exaggerated tension between Susan and her sister Rosemary (who draws a line down the middle of their bedroom) in *A Parcel of Trees* again is never stated but is always present in their speech; and the deeply felt, but again never exaggerated, affection that Robert feels for his older brother Michael in *Pig-in-the-Middle* is most movingly but economically handled. Mayne never makes the mistake of over-drawing these tensions until they become false tragedies. He knows that family life is not like that. But he has a wonderfully sure touch for the complex love-hate, friendship-dislike, need-for-yet-wanting-to-be-away-from that all close families share, and a family, though it is seldom the centre, always plays an important part in his books. He is almost but not quite as good with the relationships between children at school and at play.

The world of William Mayne is an intimate one, restricted to a few people closely observed, and circumscribed always by the normal ranging abilities of children and their inescapable necessity to report home for meals and bed and to school during term-time. It is, in fact, the true world of children. But it is in some ways a *mental* world, the projection of someone whose own deeply-felt love of childhood has never been lost, and who spins his wonderfully fine web of imaginative truth from the truth he knew rather than the truth he sees. It is a world which has something in common with Kenneth Grahame's. Not because there is any similarity between their books, but because both look backwards at childhood with an adult mind. Both are genuinely thinking hard about children, striving to get their essential nature down on paper, to tell us how they think and feel, what life seems like to them, what they think of us, to make it possible for us to share a child's world. But Kenneth Grahame never succeeded, in those of his books which are about children, in making them truly *for* children, whereas William Mayne does. His world is one which children and their parents inhabit equally and this is the second distinguishing mark of his books—that no part of them is ever included cursorily. Everything that is in them is there for a purpose and each part is handled with the same kind of observation and affection. The world of school, the world of home, the world of play are indivisible to him, they are all part of the world of childhood, and that is the world he writes about.

William Mayne has written a great many books. It is some years since I counted them, but when last I did so there were two picture-story books; three very short books for young children in the Gazelle series; four in the Antelope series; three in Reindeer books and twenty full-length novels of the kind discussed above. No writer at any time has been able to sustain such an output at the same level, and Mayne is no exception. Some of his books for younger readers are very slight, almost trivial and whatever need it is that drives him to produce this large and varied output of small books for series is clearly not the same need from which are created the bigger books. Stories such as *The Big Wheel and the Little Wheel, The Fishing Party, The Last Bus* and so on are at least as well done as any other contributor to such series would have done them, and sometimes even within these patterns he can produce a little gem like *No More School*, but it can only be regretted that a writer who is capable of *A Swarm in May, The Blue Boat, Sand, Pig-in-the-Middle* or *Earthfasts* should find it necessary to spend any of his precious time on trivialities like *Plot Night*.

A Swarm in May has already been described in the section on school stories (p. 82). He is unlikely to write a better book. It has all the Mayne qualities, fine dialogue (the way in which the characters of the different masters are brought out in discussion is remarkable) and a lovingly observed *mise-en-scène* superbly served by one of his best plots. *Sand* has also been referred to in passing in the same section. In a small town on the East Coast of England which is being overtaken by the sea and the sand a group of boys, observed with the author's usual humorous detachment, finds a buried railway line in the sand and when digging to uncover it comes across a skeleton which they first think is a dinosaur but which later turns out to be a whale. The story contains some of Mayne's best dialogue, and the talk and behaviour of the girls and boys is not only finely observed and accurately recorded but is also at times very funny. Many of Mayne's stories are set in one of these smaller coastal towns or villages, where the past is still a living one, the population is small, everyone knows everyone else and relationships are close between a small group of mostly working-class families, shopkeepers, electricians, railwaymen, painters and other tradesmen. *Pig-in-the-Middle* has much the same kind of plot. This time a group of boys find a disused mill with an old barge still afloat in the middle of the mill pond. They plan to build a cabin on it, rig it with masts and sail and journey to Holland in it. But a lamp is left alight accidentally, the barge catches fire and a serious accident is fortunately averted by the ill-organised, slightly frenzied and altogether naturally messy rescue efforts of the boys, which are, however, finally successful. But, as with *Sand*, it is not the story that matters, it is the people in it, and Michael's family is one of Mayne's best-sustained portraits. Mum, with her impatient and loving-hearted slaps; father, with his football and television; the two boys, sharing a room and just beginning to feel the inevitable division between a boy who is growing up and one who is still a child, and the daughter who is only lightly sketched in but still a very real part of the family. One of the nicest touches is the conviction of Robert, the younger boy, that his mother has forgotten Michael's birthday and is getting ready to shed him, as if he were a cub that she had licked and done with.

It is not necessary to describe more of William Mayne's plots. The theme is usually much the same in every book—though with subtle variations—and interest is sustained by the fun and liveliness of the children rather than massive doses of action. An exception is *Earthfasts*. Until this book was written William Mayne had resolutely avoided pure fantasy. Many of his books hovered on the borderline between reality and fantasy, but always at the end there proved to be a rational explanation of the strange things that occurred—sometimes to the disappointment of children, many of whom persist in believing, for example, in the unicorn in *A Grass Rope*. There are no rational explanations in *Earthfasts*. Two schoolboys, David and Keith, with clearly defined differences in character, come upon an eighteenth-century drummer-boy, lost in time after searching beneath the Castle grounds for lost Arthurian treasure. The drummer-boy carries a candle, still alight after all those centuries, and this is left to David and draws him back into the past. This is an uncanny book, with an extraordinary power of conviction that impresses one again with Mayne's great gifts. The suspension of disbelief while reading is so complete that the sense of chill that the boys experience comes through vividly. Only at the end, when many readers will reject the idea of the drummer-boy being left alive above the ground, to settle down and become an ordinary human boy again, is the reader brought up suddenly by a question. Mayne talked about this book at the 1969 Exeter Conference and the substance of what he said then is recorded in the second issue of *Children's Literature in Education*. It is interesting to note that he first thought of killing the boy off and only left him alive because others asked him to do so.

I have no wish to belittle William Mayne's work, because I think him the truest and most creative of those few major authors who are genuinely writing *for* children. But it would be a mistake to think that his books will be widely popular, or that all children will enjoy them. So much so that parents, teachers or librarians who try to force children who do not like them to read them are doing the author a real disservice. Those children who do appreciate and enjoy them will come back to them again and again, but they are always likely to be in a minority.

William Mayne's first book, *Follow the Footprints*, was published in 1953 and he won the Carnegie Medal with *A Grass Rope* in 1957, so his reputation stands on a secure, twenty-year-old foundation. Alan Garner's is more recent, his first book having been published in 1960.

Alan Garner's first book was *The Weirdstone of Brisingamen*. In this and its sequel, *The Moon of Gomrath*, he made use of much of the material of earlier attempts at creating contemporary sagas and it seemed likely at first that he was planning a sustained series. These stories of the knights bound in sleep until they can be wakened to fight the forces of evil have moments of strength, but are marred by uncertainty in their organisation, roughness in the writing and a general sense of unsureness of touch. Although they were warmly received when they were first published they are clearly prentice work and the author abandoned this vein when he moved on to stronger work. He is at his best with the natural surroundings of the stories, which are set at Alderley Edge in Cheshire, and at his worst with the children, who are not fully realised and do not come alive.

The same defect is apparent in *Elidor*, an otherwise far better book. Four children in one of the poorer districts of Manchester explore a ruined church and suddenly find themselves not transported to, but living a parallel life in the terrifying land of Elidor. The two worlds overlap and the disturbing, at times frightening, fusion of this other world and the everyday world makes this a highly original book, the effect of which is heightened by Charles Keeping's dramatic illustrations. It is interesting that Charles Keeping, in a paper in *Children's Literature in Education*,[1] should have said that he did not altogether like the book while he was illustrating it, because he didn't believe in the children.

Elidor has been a much praised book and I am going against the weight of critical opinion in saying that to me it seems a contrived one. In an article in *The Times Literary Supplement* about his work, the author said of this book:

> 'For instance, in the third book, *Elidor*, I had to read extensively textbooks on physics; Celtic symbolism; archaeology; study the writings of Jung; brush up my Plato; visit Avebury, Silbury and Coventry Cathedral; spend a lot of time with demolition gangs on slum clearance sites; and listen to the whole of Britten's *War Requiem* nearly every day. A major block in the writing was resolved by seeing Robert Stephens' performance as Atahualpa in *The Royal Hunt of the Sun* at Chichester.'

Such an approach may be admirable (the author goes on to admit that this is 'an absurd list' but clearly intends it to be taken seriously) but is not likely to produce enduring writing for children. When writers for children talk in this way of their work the suspicion is aroused that it is being written as much for adult critics to admire as for children to enjoy. An infinitely greater amount of knowledge and research lies behind *The Lord of the Rings*, but that was not research undertaken in order to write an impressive children's book. The writer already possessed the knowledge, it had become a natural part of his own culture, and its contribution to the book was no more and no less than that made by any other man's natural equipment.

It seems likely from statements that Garner has made about his writing that he works best when he can use a framework of this kind on which to build his stories—Leon Garfield has quoted him as saying that he 'uses fantasy as a crutch'.[2] Whether or not this is so, his next, and best-known book, *The Owl Service*, is based on a story in the *Mabinogion*, about Lleu Llaw Gyffes and his wife, who was made for him out of

[1] Charles Keeping in *Children's Literature in Education*, No. 1, Ward, Lock, 1970.
[2] Leon Garfield, 'Writing for Childhood', *Children's Literature in Education*, No. 2, Ward, Lock, 1970.

flowers, but who destroyed him and was then herself turned into an owl. Garner has explained that he was fascinated by this story, and turned it over in his mind for some time, but could make nothing of it until he saw somewhere a dinner service with an elaborate pattern of flowers which the owner had touched up until the model of an owl appeared. The dinner service is used as a symbol of the legend, and plays an important if at times confusing part in the story, which is essentially a modern one of tension between youth and age, class and class, Welsh and English, with powerful forces of hatred and revenge, illegitimacy and adultery brooding over the protagonists.

The figures around whom the legend repeats itself are Gwyn, whose mother lets the greater part of her large house to summer visitors; Alison and Roger, a stepbrother and sister from a higher social class, who are staying in the house with their father and mother; Gwyn's mother Nancy, and the enigmatic figure of Huw, the gardener and handyman around the house who is, we learn later, Gwyn's father. The story begins with Alison's discovery of the Owl Service when she is ill in bed. For the young people the house becomes filled with menace emanating from the service, and strange poltergeistic events, described with considerable conviction, accumulate and seem to threaten them. Gwyn, who though very much a child of Wales, wants to leave the village and become better educated, is perceptive and imaginative, shy, bookish and at times boorish. The English boy, Roger, is his antithesis and the clash between them is sharpened by jealousy over Alison, suspicion, and the fear created by inexplicable things that happen as the legend begins to work itself out.

On a first reading, especially to a reader unfamiliar with the *Mabinogion*, much of this seems inflated and insincere, but on a second reading, with the symbolism more familiar, the tension and power that the author has built into the relationships become impressive. The themes of jealousy, social distinction and past hatreds are painfully real. It is obviously a powerful and significant novel and though there is an atmosphere about it that is at times snobbish and unpleasant this is possibly intended.

The Owl Service, more than any other book for children, puts critics, librarians, teachers and everyone else professionally interested in the matter of children's reading, on their mettle. Is it, or is it not, a book suitable for children? And is it, or is it not, successful? Is it a good book? The last question is the easiest to answer simply. Yes, of course it is. It stands head and shoulders above the average book written for children and is obviously the work of a genuinely creative artist. Nevertheless it does not seem to me wholly successful. Too much is made, I feel, of the legend and the dinner service, and the author is so convincing at human relationships and the development of his characters that he could almost certainly have made as good a book, perhaps even a better one, without the elaborately contrived symbolism. I wonder, in fact, whether more than one in ten of the children who read the book even notice it. Children, as we all know, are capable of reading books at several different levels, and the application of the legend is so involved and the incidents in which it is worked out so complex that they must be difficult for any but the most intelligent and widely read child to follow. I suspect, therefore, that they don't even try, and that most children read this simply as a story about people, aware no doubt of a kind of horrid and unnatural fascination that they find emotionally and sensually disturbing, which attracts them to the book without being understood, but largely unaware of the fact that the author has an underlying purpose.

That the book has a fascination is undeniable. Aidan Chambers, in his study of *The Reluctant Reader*, has described its success with a class of not specially intelligent fourth-formers, and it seems to me that he makes his point about communication without necessarily explicit understanding convincingly and well.

It will be very interesting to see along what lines Alan Garner develops his work. Having aroused so much controversy and attracted so much critical interest so early in his career he must inevitably feel the need to live up to it. He is unlikely, therefore, ever to turn to a simpler kind of writing. But it cannot be altogether healthy for a writer for children to be so conscious of the need to be intelligent, different, challenging—the need always to produce a new work that is more demanding than the last. It is this obvious perfectionism that makes him so unusual even among his contemporaries. He takes his craft very seriously, gives far more time to each book than the majority of present-day writers and has probably given more thought to the theory and practice of writing for children than anyone else. The article that he wrote for *The Times Literary Supplement* has already been referred to. Anyone genuinely interested in studying the development of a significant writer—or the future of writing for children generally—would be well advised to look up and study this article. For in it he not only had a good deal to say about how he came to write *The Owl Service* and other books but he also gives a convincing, and illuminating, account of his own creative process.[1]

If thinking were all that is necessary to make a good book, Alan Garner would undoubtedly in time produce some of the best children's books ever written. But loving is at least as important, and in this quality he seems less well endowed. If only it were possible to graft William Mayne's gift for dialogue, humour and loving-hearted observation on to Alan Garner's creative intelligence what a fine book would result!

There is, I feel, more in common between Mayne and Garner than is immediately apparent. Both write, in the main, from within themselves rather than from direct observation of children; both write for themselves, rather than for children (whose good fortune comes as a by-product); and both love, and live in, country places, living their own lives in their own ways. The list could be extended, but where they may well separate is in their future developments. William Mayne, I am sure, will always write about children, for that is where his heart and mind is. Alan Garner *may* continue to do so, but it is at least equally likely that his inquiring mind may in time need something stronger to test itself on and that he will then turn to writing equally demanding novels for adults.

Although William Mayne and Alan Garner have been dealt with at length, as especially interesting and important, there has been an astonishing growth of new writers of stature since 1950 and it is not possible to give special treatment to them all. But the forces that have influenced the development of the main stream of children's writing in Britain during the last decade can be seen at work in their clearest and most direct form in the novels of K. M. Peyton. Beginning rather shakily, with a number of undistinguished adventure stories, she first showed her real gifts in a series of stories about the sea near the Essex coast, *Windfall*, *The Maplin Bird*, and *The Plan for Birdsmarsh*. These were notable for fine descriptive writing about the sea and sailing, excellently observed characterisation, and well-thought-out plots, but were not essentially different, other than in quality, from other books of their kind. In *Thunder in the Sky* she tackled the more difficult subject of the conflicts in the mind

[1] Alan Garner, 'A Bit More Practice', *Times Literary Supplement*, June 6, 1968.

of a fifteen-year-old boy involved in the First World War—
though still with the assured background of the sea and sailing
to help her. *Fly-By-Night*, her only story for younger children, though it can be read on one level as just another pony
story, is at the same time a realistic and obviously genuinely-
felt study of the social problems in new communities—an
interesting example of a writer using a well-tried theme and
familiar personal material to support a move closer to reality.
(A somewhat similar example of this can be seen in the later
books of Vian Smith, a lesser writer but one who combined in
much the same way a love of horses with a genuine feeling for
character and some understanding of social problems, as for
example in *Come Down the Mountain*.)

Drawing by Victor Ambrus for Flambards in Summer, *by
K. M. Peyton (Oxford University Press).*

In K. M. Peyton's next book, *Flambards*, a story of a young girl growing up in Edwardian England, the thrills and pleasures of riding are still there, but they have taken their proper place in the development of what becomes, especially in the later books, *The Edge of the Cloud* and *Flambards in Summer*, virtually a realistic novel. In the final volume of the trilogy action has been reduced to a minimum and interest is sustained instead by the development of Christina's character under stress. A list of the social problems involved might give the impression that this is yet another of those deliberately contrived 'social realism' stories, but in fact what makes this the almost perfect prototype of one kind of children's novel of the future is the skill with which the author tackles such problems as pregnancy, illegitimacy, and ill-matched love genuinely yet without ever becoming too emotionally involved, or too complex for children of the age for which she is writing. *Flambards in Summer* made clear the course on which the author was set, so it was not unexpected that her next book, *Pennington's Seventeenth Summer*, should be a study of near-delinquency. The theme of the maverick seventeen-year-old is a difficult one and though this is a compulsively readable book it does not completely convince. Reginald Maddock's *The Pit*, though infinitely less sophisticated and about a younger boy, comes much nearer to the truth and makes an interesting comparison.

More time has been spent on K. M. Peyton than can be given to other writers mentioned later because she is such an interesting example of what we can expect for the future from writing for children. It is unlikely that she will ever write a masterpiece, but she is a sophisticated, highly intelligent, and well-organised writer making the most of her powers, and children will be fortunate indeed if they are given many books like hers. She is also a talented artist, and has illustrated several of her own books—in a way that is completely different from the Arthur Ransome accuracy-above-all type of author-illustrator.

Anne Barrett, like Philippa Pearce, writes both realism and fantasy and her best book, *Midway*, is a fantasy and has already been discussed. *Songberd's Grove*, however, is a book which has been widely praised for its social realism. This story about life as it is alleged to be lived in a *déclassé* London street no doubt began as a determined attempt to paint an authentic picture, but one suspects that the author's natural zest soon overtook her and the story degenerates (or improves, according to one's taste) into a delightfully fantastic dream of real life, with an ex-Spanish dancer, an architect *deus ex machina* and even, in the end, a lovable old nobleman who puts everything to rights. But despite the completely improbable, wish-fulfilment plot, the story is real in its own way and children enjoy it without question—so perhaps after all it does tell them something about life in *Songberd's Grove*. Anne Barrett is another writer who takes a long time between books and her output is even more limited than Philippa Pearce's. How sad it is that writers whose books are, on the whole, worthless, produce them like sausages out of a machine, whereas the real artists among children's writers (with odd exceptions like William Mayne) write so few.

Books like *Songberd's Grove* were the forerunners of the modern realistic story for children in Britain. There has been a much longer tradition of realistic writing in the United States, which is probably why writers on that side of the Atlantic seem to have found it easier to write simply and naturally about everyday life (as they do also, of course, in Australia) without the too obvious straining after an effect that mars much of British writing of this kind. Too many such books have been over-praised for their themes, without proper notice having been taken of their quality. Josephine Kamm's books, such as *Young Mother* and *Out of Step*, lack any real depth (the former is almost a textbook on how to have an illegitimate child and the latter skirts all the real problems of its theme of love between black and white). Reginald Taylor's *The Boy from Hackston N.E.* is as with-it as today—and will probably be forgotten tomorrow; and though there are better books, like Janet McNeill's *The Battle of St George Without* or Richard Parker's *The Punch Back Gang*, their titles and production styles are becoming so similar that it is difficult to tell them apart.

Telling them apart seems not, in fact, to be wanted, because many of the best known of them are now appearing in series, with similar production styles and jackets. Series like Topliners serve a useful purpose, but they are a perplexing problem for anyone trying to assess books written for children by familiar literary standards. We are back to McLuhan again, with his attacks on literacy. Books like these, presumably, are not intended for the literate, but to encourage 'under achievers' to read. It is depressing that such books should find their way into libraries in schools where they are not really needed, and where their easiness and accessibility may tempt children who are capable of reading better books into wasting their time on them. They are in many ways the modern equivalent of the 'Peg's Paper' type of novelette, that forty or fifty years ago used to be regarded, snobbishly, as for those who knew nothing better—but which were probably read surreptitiously by a far wider public. They are, in fact, nearer to light romantic reading than to true realism.

This is not the place for a full-length study of *that* issue, but a critic should be prepared to nail his colours to the mast, so it should be said that I do not believe that the author who sets out with the intention of 'dealing' with a specific social problem is ever likely to produce a first-class book. Any more than I believe in any other deliberately-contrived work. It *is* possible for an imaginative and creative novel to be true to life, but it is impossible for the *planned* realistic novel—the one that sets out deliberately to deal with illegitimacy, or drug-taking, or some other currently fashionable topic, to be truly imaginative and creative.

This is not an attempt to argue that realistic books are unnecessary, or to deny that they serve any useful purpose. A truly realistic book can serve a very useful purpose indeed. For we live in a complex and troubled society and those growing up into it, who will have to carry its burdens into the future, need help. Children at the age at which difficulties first begin to seem insurmountable tend to be introspective; perplexed by puberty and their growing awareness of new aspects of life; shy of others, and diffident of approaching adults. Books offer them the best way of finding out for themselves the things they need to know. A book can be taken away into one's bedroom, or to a quiet corner of the garden, and pondered over free from prying eyes and the jeering comments of friends or family.

This is the age at which a true creative writer, working under a genuine compulsion to produce an honest book on a difficult topic can be the best friend a child could have. But those who write glibly for children, without themselves knowing truly what they mean (or without themselves possessing any genuine sense of values), confusing moral issues, and twisting both character and incident to contrive solutions that are temporarily acceptable but leave no lasting satisfaction in their readers' minds—such writers are doing children a grave disservice. And those who encourage them are equally to blame.

This debate goes back a long way. It has its roots nearly

thirty years ago, in the early comments of critics who thought the time had come when children's books needed a change of scene, that children needed to have their horizons enlarged. As a result we praised too highly *The Family From One End Street*, not because we thought it good, but because it was all we could find of that sort to praise—the early stories of Howard Spring having gone unnoticed. Unhappily the shadow of One End Street hangs over much contemporary realistic writing for children. That basically unreal, snobbish, unsatisfying book has a lot to answer for.

Among the heirs of One End Street-ism have been too many books like Elizabeth Stucley's over-praised *Magnolia Buildings* which, like *One End Street*, is an outside-looking-in book that is basically snobbish, because the reader is aware all the time—as the writer too obviously was—that a lower order of beings is under observation. As writers improve their techniques and become more assured in their treatment of such topics, this particularly distasteful form of realism will disappear, or at least lessen, but we are unlikely to get truly realistic books of this sort until a new class of writer emerges —one which can, from personal knowledge, look from the inside at the outside, instead of the other way round.

Drawing by Eve Garnett for her book The Family From One End Street (*Frederick Muller*).

There are a few writers who come near to this. Frederick Grice's *The Oak and the Ash*, a grimly realistic story of life in a Durham colliery village, is probably as near to actual truth as such books can ever become but it is doubtful whether children will enjoy it, or whether indeed this is the kind of book that the advocates of social realism want.

Nearer to a successful combination of the realities of life and a sufficiently sustained plot to hold the young reader's interest, is Reginald Maddock's *The Pit*. Reginald Maddock is the headmaster of a school in the north of England and this story about Butch Reece, the difficult son of a drunken father but loving mother and sister in an industrial town on the edge of the moors, shows real understanding of children and their motives—at least to the depth at which it is either necessary or desirable at their reading age. It is a better and truer book than many that have been praised more highly for their realism. Reginald Maddock has written two other books about the same area, *The Dragon in the Garden* and *Sell-out*. His solutions are perhaps a little too easily come by, but these are books for children, not books for critics, and children on the whole prefer solutions which they can understand, without too much involved and introspective examination of character and motive.

Barbara Willard is another writer who is capable at her best of a naturalness that is as near to the truth of life as most young readers want to get. *Charity at Home* is a moving story of an orphaned girl growing up in a strange home with an uncle and aunt with whom she feels out of touch. *The House with Roots*, *Eight for a Secret* and *The Battle of Wednesday Week* all have contemporary themes. She is an uneven writer, who is better known for her historical novels than these more conventional stories, but her books have an honest simplicity that is very attractive to children.

There are a number of writers at about this level whose quality is as yet uncertain. An unexpected one is Joan G. Robinson, whose Teddy Robinson books have already been mentioned. She has recently produced a couple of books, *When Marnie was There* (already discussed on page 118) and *Charley*, which reveal an interesting and unusual approach. *Charley* is the story of a child who, feeling herself unwanted, and presented with an opportunity to hide for a time from life, takes it and lives by herself in a field for nearly a week. It sounds an absurd plot, put baldly, but the author makes it convincing, avoids sentimentality and has produced a moving book.

Illustration by Dick Hart for Gumble's Yard, *by John Rowe Townsend (Hutchinson).*

Antonia Forest's books about the Marlow family and Margaret Storey's *Pauline* have already been mentioned. A survival from an earlier period is Elfrida Vipont, whose *The Lark on the Wing*, the second book in her trilogy about the Haverards, was a Carnegie Medal winner in 1950 and a forerunner to the 'new look' in children's books. Her books are natural and readable but only really come to life when someone is singing, or playing, or talking about music.

Among the male writers two stand out, John Rowe Townsend and Philip Turner, and they make an interesting comparison. Philip Turner's books are cast in a conventional mould, nearer to the Ransome tradition than any other contemporary writer of stature, but they are redeemed by accurate and affectionate observation of children; their dialogue is good and their plots are well organised and cleverly sustain excitement without introducing anything sensational.

John Rowe Townsend, on the other hand, is completely up to date. Like K. M. Peyton, he has developed over a number of books, until his control over his intentions is assured and sustained. His novels, which are usually about the backgrounds and lives of children from the poorest kind of home, are well written and seemingly based on close observation, and their well-organised plots usually include some theme of interest to those who seek for 'socially conscious' novels for children. But this aspect of them is not over-stressed and he is the most successful of the recent 'realistic' writers, because his earlier books can be read at a different level simply as straight and thoroughly exciting adventure stories. Children, therefore, do enjoy them. These are still outside-looking-in books, and though they avoid snobbishness the reader is left aware that they are the results of observation rather than experience, but they are as good as this kind is likely to be. Children may never be able to learn how the children of poor homes with limited opportunities and difficult backgrounds really feel, until one of them grows up and becomes a good writer for them. Until that happens the best we can hope for is that intelligent writers, who look hard at what they see and try genuinely to understand, will do their honest best to observe and interpret. This is where writers like John Rowe Townsend are so valuable, and this is why his work is so interesting. His earlier books, though their backgrounds were unusual, were not so very different in kind from lesser stories of adventure. Mysterious strangers, mis-understandings, children in conflict with dishonesty, many of the conventional ingredients were used to give interest to his plots though he never allowed them to conflict with the main issues of character that he was really concerned with. But his later work has deepened and strengthened and is noticeably tending towards an older age level.

Good-night, Prof, Love is a subtly planned story of ado-lescence. The seventeen-year-old lower middle class anti-hero is the son of a small town accountant. Nearing the end of his grammar school education, he has avoided the local girls because he prefers to daydream of graceful upper class girls with pleasanter voices. Freed for a week from his too-possessive mother, he comes accidentally in contact with a waitress in a café and although she is the antithesis of his dream girls, he is rendered defenceless by his lack of experience and becomes emotionally involved with her. The girl welcomes the opportunity to escape from her own diffi-culties and runs away with him. After they have spent some nights together she is instrumental in returning him to his family. This summary of the plot will indicate how remote the book is from earlier children's books. The story is not, in fact, distasteful (except for those who find any discussion of sex distasteful) for what could have been its seamy aspects are ingeniously avoided by the fact that it is all told in dialogue. There is almost no description, no author's asides, and the reader is left to deduce character and motivation from what is said. But is it a 'children's book'? And, even if it is, will children continue to read such books when novels like David Storey's *This Sporting Life* or Keith Waterhouse's *Billy Liar* are available to them, which are not children's books, do not look like children's books, but are easy to read and can tell them perhaps more about true realism than most children's books?

As anyone over fifty will have realised, *Good-night, Prof, Love* is, in effect, a late twentieth-century de-glamorised version of Warwick Deeping's *Sorrell and Son*. That was an adult book, but sixteen-year-old boys read it and no doubt learnt as much from it, though in a different way, as they will from *Good-night, Prof, Love*. No serious adult novelist would write *Sorrell and Son* or its equivalent today. Can it be that books like John Rowe Townsend's and Alan Garner's have become necessary to take the place of a kind of adult novel that has disappeared? Are we witnessing the birth of a new kind of book, that is neither a children's book nor an adult novel, but something in between? And are writers like Alan Garner, K. M. Peyton, Stephanie Plowman and John Rowe Townsend the forerunners of this new genre? If they are, there will be some interesting problems for publishers, editors and designers, because a new production style will have to be evolved. Stephanie Plowman's books, for example, although they are not illustrated, have jackets that are no different in general style from the jackets of many other historical novels for children. John Rowe Townsend's book is both illustrated and has a picture jacket of a 'children's book' kind. *The Owl Service*, significantly, has no internal illustrations and a dignified jacket that would not be out of place on an adult novel, though, in some indefinable way it still looks like a children's book—perhaps it is the publisher's general setting style that achieves this effect? What publishers will have to evolve is a style that distinguishes this new kind of 'novel for young adults' both from other children's books—and from adult books. A style which will be attractive to young readers without carrying the distinguishing (and thus pejorative) mark of a 'children's book', but which is not so different in general appearance from an adult book that adult readers, in their turn, will not feel that it is beneath them.

Conclusion

British writing for children has come a long way in the twentieth century, and in the past twenty years has made impressive progress. The sub-culture of indistinguishable third-rate reading persists—anyone who believes that the kind of book for children discussed here has yet penetrated to any depth should spend a day in a big wholesaler's showroom, or study a list of annuals, of which there are still some hundreds produced. But that is no longer any fault of the writers or, be it said to their credit, of the majority of responsible publishers. Better children's books now exist in sufficient variety, in levels of comprehension, reading and appeal, for any child to enjoy. British writers for children have in the past twenty years produced some of the best literature for children of any age, and there is promise of as good work to come.

Only two dangers threaten the future. The first is that we should become complacent and fail to make the determined efforts that are still needed to break through the comprehension barrier between those who care and those who mindlessly continue to believe that it does not matter *what* children read, or even if they read at all, so long as they have something to keep them quiet for a time, and out of mischief. The second danger is that, in our efforts to break this barrier, we may go too far the other way, towards the newer didacticism that is already apparent on the horizon.

Forty years ago hardly anyone outside a small group of specialists cared seriously about children's books and almost no one wrote about them. There was no platform for informed opinion on them in the national press—apart from an occasional piece at Christmas—and it is difficult to imagine the public, in those days, being even at all interested in what a writer for children had to say about his work. Today so many people, of so many different interests, are involved in children's books; so many people write about them; and so many authors give lectures, write articles and attend seminars on their works, that the subject is in danger of being overworked. And it is all so very serious.

The way to attract new readers, or reluctant readers, to reading is not to make reading solemn. Reading should always be enjoyable. It is not a religion, or a school subject, or a form of education (though it can be a part of all these things). It is a leisure art, an enjoyable exercise of man's mind and an uplift for his spirit, of the same kind as music, or theatre, or poetry, or any other art. None of these things has any life if it does not give pleasure; though that pleasure can be of many kinds, some easy, some hard, and though those that in the end leave us best satisfied are often those which stretch us most.

It will be easier for writers to avoid both these dangers if the status of children's writing can be further improved, to the point at which the still-remaining artificial distinction between 'children's books' and 'books' can be broken down. Though there has been a great advance in the past decade, the distinction remains. Writers of children's books still achieve little recognition in any but their own highly specialised professional circle, and writers about children's books are still regarded, consciously or unconsciously, as a kind of sub-species of critic—doing a secondary task from which the more successful among them may one day hope to be promoted to more responsible work. It is significant that *The Times Literary Supplement*, though giving more space to children's books over the year than any other reviewing journal, has yet to include a review of any children's books in its own annual anthology of reviews. The nearest it ever came to that was the inclusion, in *T.L.S.* 3 in 1962, of a review of a minor pamphlet, George H. Pumphrey's *What Children Think of Their Comics*, an inclusion which may be thought almost as enlightening as the omissions.

The best of British children's books are a significant part of our literature and culture and they deserve and should be given adequate recognition, at a level which will encourage writers to do the best work of which they are capable, and parents and others to appreciate that they can be measured by recognisable standards of taste and discrimination. Too many parents, unhappily, are still neglectful of their children's reading. They think that if they have sent them to a good school, given them a comfortable room, plenty of food and the kind of leisure enjoyments that they want, this is enough. But it is not. A good school, certainly, is an important factor—if it is the kind of school that is aware of other things than the necessity to pass 'A' levels—but how many parents know much about what their children learn at school, and the way it is being taught? Fewer still have any interest at all in what they read.

A parent who has only provided for the material side of his children's welfare has only done half his job. All parents should ask themselves constantly, 'What have we given our children?' 'What effort have we made to pass on to them the culture that we inherited and to help them to go a step further and become more aware than we were of what art, literature and music can give us?' Parents who have read widely themselves have a special duty here, because the probabilities are that they will know more about the books that exist than their children's teachers. They should not too readily assume that their children will acquire at school, from their friends, or by some undisclosed process of osmosis the same knowledge of the life of literature that they themselves possess. Things are different now. School life is more arduous; there is a great deal of highly specialised knowledge to acquire, and very little time, either in the curriculum or in children's limited leisure, for what I recently heard a science teacher describe with contempt as 'descriptive' reading. The child who is exposed, naturally, as a normal part of a happy home life, to the best work of good writers, is fortunate indeed. And the best way to achieve this is of course to give him books which have been chosen with care and to influence uncles and aunts and anyone else who gives him books to do the same.

Every parent who is at least intelligent enough to be able to make value judgements about the things which are important to him should realise that the books which he gives to his children should be selected in the same way. Until he does so only a minority of the children in this country will be given the opportunity to read the best of the books described here.

Appendix A

Regional Writing

In the past twenty years there has been an increase in regional writing of various kinds. 'Books about other countries' have become fashionable and although many of these have been commissioned—too often written for series by writers without personal experience of the countries they are describing—local and national 'schools' of children's writing have also appeared.

The works of Irish writers, such as Patricia Lynch's fantasies and stories of everyday life, and Eilís Dillon's contemporary adventure stories, have already been mentioned. There is also a strong Scottish school. Allan Campbell McLean's adventure stories and Mollie Hunter's fantasies have been described. Other writers also use the island of Skye—so many that there can hardly be a square inch of that island on which some fictional event has not taken place. Not all of them, however, are sensational. Margaret MacPherson's stories of crofters have an earthy reality that is convincing and *The Rough Road* is a well-constructed and believable story of a misunderstood boy living with unsympathetic foster-parents and wrestling with the problems of adolescence. It is interesting to compare this book with Reginald Maddock's *The Pit* and K. M. Peyton's *Pennington's Seventeenth Summer*.

Iona McGregor has written a number of stories on Scottish historical themes that are notable for the excellence of their writing and good characterisation; Honor Arundel writes pleasantly natural realistic stories about everyday life in Scotland and R. E. Jackson has wit and style that may one

161

day produce an outstanding book. *Aunt Eleanor* is a Ransome-ish mixture of real and imagined excitements—the supposed spies and the mysterious submarine turn out to be naturalists protecting a perhaps equally unlikely lake monster.

But the greatest development has come from Commonwealth countries. In the period since the Second World War the works of Australian and Canadian writers for children have at last begun to reach an international audience. Both countries had produced children's writing many years earlier, but much of it was derivative; it was often published overseas and too much of it concentrated on unusual aspects of their own countries for the benefit of readers in others. Only Norman Lindsay's *The Magic Pudding* and Ethel Turner's *Seven Little Australians* from Australia, and Charles G. D. Roberts's and Ernest Seton Thompson's Canadian animal stories, became widely known. The past twenty years have seen a dramatic change. In both countries the quality of the writing has strengthened; local publishing industries have developed to the stage at which most of the important books for children are published nationally; and the writers have felt able to write for their own children rather than those of other countries. There are still too many Aborigines in Australian books and too many Eskimoes in Canadian ones, and an overseas reader would still get a wrong impression from such books of the proportions of Australians and Canadians who live in cities rather than on the land, but the better writers are at last beginning to write naturally and freely about the normal everyday life of their own countries.

Australia

The first Australian book for children, *A Mother's Offering to her Children* by Lady Gordon Bremer, was published in 1841, but Ethel Turner's *Seven Little Australians*, published in 1894, was the first Australian children's book to be read overseas. Since over a million copies have been sold, many children in other countries must have formed their first ideas of Australia from it. Although Ethel Turner's books are now dated, she was an honest writer, doing her best to report accurately, and within the standards of the time her books were realistic. So the picture derived from them would not have been too false.

Illustration by Norman Lindsay for his book The Magic Pudding (*Angus and Robertson*).

The only early Australian children's book that has not dated is Norman Lindsay's *The Magic Pudding*. First published in 1918 and written, if the eighty-nine-year-old author's account in 1969 is to be taken seriously, for a bet, this is so far the one authentic Australian classic of children's writing. As John Hetherington[1] has said 'Roughly stated, the theme is eating and fighting, which is child psychology at its simplest'. But this vigorously written story of the pudding which grew again as fast as it was eaten and became extremely ill-tempered if appetites were poor, is much more than that. It is one of the great fantasies of children's literature. Told naturally and unaffectedly, at breathless speed, with an unforgettable set of characters brought superbly to life as much by the author's unaffected prose as by his even better illustrations, this is story telling at its best. Since it was first published in 1918 it has remained constantly in print and over 100,000 copies have been sold, but it is still less well known in England than it should be. There is something so unmistakably Australian about it that it makes a refreshing change from the host of pseudo-Winnie-The-Poohs and Flopsy Bunnies.

The period between the two wars produced nothing of lasting value, but soon after the Second World War a new school of writers emerged. The Australian Children's Book of the Year award was founded in 1946 (the same year as the Canadian one). It was given originally by the Australian Book Society; in 1951 it was adopted by the New South Wales Children's Book Council; in 1957 the two Children's Book Councils of New South Wales and Victoria combined to share the judging for the award, which thus became a joint one for those States; and finally in 1959 an all-Australian Children's Book Council was formed and took over the award. In 1967 the Australian Commonwealth Literary Fund for the first time added a grant of $500 to the award for the winning author, and these annual grants have so far continued. These changes give some indication of the development of interest and the moves made to increase interest in better books for children over these years. As in other countries, the existence of some form of recognition for children's writing brought about an almost immediate improvement in the general standard.

[1] John Hetherington, *Norman Lindsay*, Australian Writers and their Work, second edition 1970, OUP.

The first of the new school of Australian children's writers was Nan Chauncy, with her natural but exciting stories of the Tasmanian countryside. Her work steadily improved and deepened and her later books, especially *Tangara*, with its haunting illustrations by Brian Wildsmith, became internationally known and were reprinted in many languages.

Other writers soon followed: Joan Phipson with her pleasantly natural stories of the New South Wales outback; Patricia Wrightson, with a somewhat wider range, who has recently produced a moving story about a handicapped boy, '*I Own the Racecourse*', that is one of the better books of recent years; and Eleanor Spence, whose more sophisticated stories, though nearer in style and treatment to the now accepted type of 'Librarian's book', are nevertheless in their own way equally Australian, and equally realistic. She has attempted serious historical writing in a way that is new for Australia, and *The Switherby Pilgrims* and its sequel *Jamberoo Road* are the best work of this kind that Australia has yet produced.

Drawing by Margaret Horder for The Family Conspiracy, *by Joan Phipson (Longman).*

British Children's Books in the Twentieth Century

It is noticeable that whereas in Britain the best writing for children tends to be in the field of fantasy, in Australia it is in realism. Australian writers for children seem naturally to turn to writing about everyday life and the best recent books have been of this kind. Fantasy is rare. The only successful near-fantasy has been Randolph Stow's delightful *Midnite,* a successful take-off of all bushranging stories that is at the same time a gaily exciting adventure story. Even Aboriginal legends—Australia's nearest approach to the fairy and folk tales of older countries—though published in a number of forms seem not to arouse the interest that, for example, Indian and Eskimo folk tales do in Canada. Perhaps it is a case of first things first, and of writers in a newer country feeling the need to explore the land and its people first, before spending time on wilder flights of imagination. Whatever the cause, realism is well served in Australian children's writing; some of the best contemporary realistic writing is by Australian authors, and it seems possible that if a serious work of the 'social realism' kind now being so strongly advocated *can* at the same time be made a book that will appeal to children, it may well come from an Australian author. Colin Thiele's books about South Australian country life have not yet achieved the international reputation of some other Australian books, but they are sensitive and moving stories which reveal a deep understanding of boys and their nature and contain vivid descriptions of lovingly observed birds, animals and natural surroundings that deserve to be known more widely. Reginald Ottley's *Yamboorah* books are almost as good. Better known overseas and already reprinted in a number of languages are H. F. Brinsmead's unusually varied stories of different aspects of Australian country and city life. Her first book, *Pastures of the Blue Crane,* dealt remarkably successfully and convincingly with the problems faced by a sixteen-year-old girl who inherits a run-down banana plantation, insists on trying to make a success of it, and finally triumphs over a succession of setbacks, including the belated discovery that she is of part coloured blood. H. F. Brinsmead's books are all about adolescent girls and they are among the best examples of the newer type of children's book, which bridges the gap between the children's book proper and adult reading. *Beat of the City* dealt not altogether convincingly but courageously with under-privileged adolescents in Melbourne. Her later books are tending to become slightly 'fey', but she is the most promising of the new school of Australian writers.

Already established, and with a growing international reputation, is the best-known Australian children's writer, Ivan Southall. His books have won many awards in Australia, America and other countries, and have been translated into many languages. He is the only Australian writer to have become the subject of major reviews and discussion overseas. His stories lack the polish and sophistication of the best overseas books, but in his direct, brusque style and forthright exposition of difficult themes, coupled with compelling story telling, seem to be concentrated all the strengths and few of the weaknesses of the Australian character. At his best he is one of the few living writers for children who can still tell an exciting story compulsively. He is a born story teller, whose work developed from flying adventure stories of the simplest kind to the fine *Hills End*, a superb story, full of complex relationships, changes of heart and other subtleties, which though clearly drawn are never allowed to hold back the breathless action. *Ash Road* is almost as good, but *To the Wild Sky* suffers from a curious ambivalence that weakens it as a book for children, though it remains an impressive piece of work. The first part of the book, after some preliminary sketching in of characters, becomes a hold-on-to-your-seats account of a nightmare flight, ending in a crash on a beach. In the second half there is virtually no action and the book becomes a study of the interplay of character between the five children.

The going is as tough for the characters in Ivan Southall's novels as it often is for his readers. In *Finn's Folly* young people are involved in the consequence of a disastrous car accident; in *The Fox Hole* it is the greed of adults that threatens them; in *Chinaman's Reef is Ours* the disaster is for the first time not a physical one—neither a natural disaster nor an accident—but the taking over of an outback town by a new mining company; in *Let the Balloon Go* a spastic boy is in trouble at the top of an eighty-foot tree.

The central problem with Ivan Southall's later work, and the one that makes it so interesting to those concerned with possible developments in children's writing, is his seeming preoccupation with problems of character, and the relationship between parents and children. Those critics who have complained of the absence of parents from children's books can take a kind of comfort from Ivan Southall's books, in which parents are all too present, sometimes deplorably.

What interests readers of his books is whether children, at the age at which books like this are still read, are really at all interested, in any depth, in this sort of introspective examination of the whys and wherefores of human behaviour. They are certainly interested to some extent, but it is doubtful whether they are prepared to accept it as the central theme of a book that they will read for enjoyment. His most recent book, *Bread and Honey*, will test them strongly on this point, because it is primarily concerned with character. There is a single dramatic incident, the fight with the bully's crony, but the other elements of the book are more important, and some of them are difficult, and (in the unresolved state in which the author leaves them) unsatisfactory elements in a book of this kind. It is to be hoped that so fine a story teller is not being tempted towards fashionable themes by critical comment on 'realism'.

Canada

Although Canadian writing for children can make a claim that has been as yet denied to Australia—that her writers invented a new kind of children's book—there are curious similarities between the history of writing for children in the two countries.

The first Australian children's book was published in 1841; the first Canadian one, *Canadian Crusoes* by Catharine Parr Traill, in 1852. There was a similar failure of creative writing for children in both countries in the early part of the century; both countries launched Book Awards simultaneously in 1946/7; and in both countries a new flowering of children's literature after the war was associated with the development of local publishing.

R. M. Ballantyne, though not a Canadian, was the first writer for children to live and work in Canada. After spending six years with the Hudson Bay Company he wrote a number of books based on his Canadian experiences. *Ungava* is the only one of these now remembered, but the books established a style of Canadian adventure story that flourished for many years. In 1897 Marshall Saunders achieved phenomenal success with *Beautiful Joe*, a tear-jerking story about a handicapped dog in the tradition of *Black Beauty*, but the first Canadian children's books to achieve international success were the realistic animal stories of Ernest Seton Thompson and Charles G. D. Roberts. These stories-which were a world away from any previous use of animals in children's books, either as talking animals or as adjuncts to a child's adventures— established a new genre and were widely copied throughout the world. As Sheila Egoff[1] has shown, the strength of these books, as with so many of the best children's books, sprang from truth. When Seton and Roberts wrote their books the life of animals was an important matter to many people in a sparsely populated country, and knowledge of them and their ways was valuable. The books of both were based on close observation and study and set a pattern which later writers in England and other countries followed. As have, of course,

[1] Sheila Egoff, *The Republic of Childhood*, OUP, 1967.

later Canadian writers, the best known of whom was George Stansfield Belaney, or 'Grey Owl'. His single children's book, *The Adventures of Sajo and her Beaver People*, was published in 1935, thirty years after Roberts' first collection of stories. Seton Thompson's first collection appeared in 1898.

After Seton Thompson and Roberts the next Canadian children's writer to achieve an international reputation was L. M. Montgomery, whose *Anne of Green Gables*, published in 1908, became a world best-seller and, unlike *Seven Little Australians*, is still widely read. In 1936 another romantic story, Muriel Denison's *Susannah, A Little Girl with the Mounties*, achieved temporarily a wide reputation at a time when *Rose Marie* had made the Mounties fashionable.

But the real strength of Canadian writing for children continued to be in the Thompson and Roberts strain, and in 1931 Roderick Haig-Brown, who was to become one of Canada's best known children's writers, published *Silver: The Life of an Atlantic Salmon*, followed in 1934 by *Ki-Yu: A Story of Panthers*, a grimly realistic story that makes few concessions. Roderick Haig-Brown later turned to fiction and in stories such as *Starbuck Valley Winter* and *Saltwater Summer* produced a number of tales based on close personal knowledge and observation and a great feeling for landscape and sense of place. A deep love of country plays an important part in Canadian writing for children, something that is lacking in Australian children's writing, for though much of that is *about* the Australian countryside the writers seem not to have felt the same sense of love and involvement. At times it seems almost as if they hated it.

Another significant Canadian writer for children, Farley Mowat, also wrote about animals. His *The Dog who Wouldn't Be* and *Owls in the Family* were read equally by children and adults. They are a long way from Ernest Seton Thompson but in their own way as closely observed—and remarkably funny. *Never Cry Wolf*, a later book published in 1963, was nearer to the earlier tradition in that it resulted from close observation of wolf life, but it is only incidentally a children's story. It was written for a specific purpose, but makes nevertheless an absorbing book of interest to everyone, child or adult, who cares about the survival of wild things in their natural surroundings.

Writing about animals and wild things seems to come most naturally to Canadian writers, because the next two books worth mention were also of this kind. Fred Bodsworth's *Last of the Curlews* is an account of the migration of curlews from the Arctic to the grasslands of South America, a realistic study that contains too little that is romantic to be generally popular. Sheila Burnford's *The Incredible Journey*, on the other hand, contains almost too much. This much-loved story of two dogs and a cat who make a 250-mile trek through the wild of northern Ontario to return home has become an international best-seller, has been successfully filmed, and must be one of the best-known Canadian stories.

It is interesting to compare the Canadian and Australian award winners for the past twenty years. If the Canadian judges are right, and there seems no reason why they should not be, Canadian writers in recent years have produced a number of fine collections of folk and other tales (*Glooskap's Country, Tales of Nanabozhi, The Double Knights* and so on), some interesting factual books, legends, collections of verse and other miscellanea, but they have not as yet produced a school of writers of fiction in any way comparable with the Australian realistic writers. Canadian fiction for children, it seems, has yet to take its place in the main stream of British children's writing.

New Zealand

The relative paucity of New Zealand writing for children emphasises the close relationship between the development of a local publishing industry and the production of national books for children. Publishing in New Zealand has been slow to develop. A small population and a particularly strong book trade association with Great Britain, resulting in a greater than usual reliance on British books, have combined to limit the production of books of purely local interest and there has thus been little demand to encourage New Zealand writing for children. The pioneer work of Dorothy Ballantyne (Neal White) has been widely admired and New Zealand children's libraries have been strongly developed, but this 'quantity circulation of quality books' has not as yet encouraged many New Zealand books. An award for the best New Zealand Children's Book of the Year was founded in 1945—a year before either Australia or Canada—in honour of Esther Glen, a New Zealand author of stories and poems for children. But this has so far been awarded five times only, in 1945, 1947, 1950, 1959 and 1964.

An unusual feature of New Zealand writing for children has been the part played by the School Publications Branch of the Education Department. Peter Wells described this remarkable work in 1957[1] and the Department has continued to play an important part in the production of New Zealand writing for children—a part that would become less significant if there were more domestic publishing. New Zealand must be the only country in the world, certainly the only country in the English-speaking world, in which the best writing for children has appeared in official publications. Maurice Duggan's *Falter Tom and the Water Boy*, the 1959 Esther Glen Award winner, was first published by the School Publications Branch, as were also Roderick Finlayson's *Springing Fern*, and a distinguished photographic picture book *The Wind and the Rain* (1966). Nevertheless there are inevitable editorial restraints on official publications and this

[1] Peter Wells, *The New Zealand School Publications Branch*, Unesco, 1957. Educational Studies and Documents No 25.

must have a limiting effect, as was apparent when there was a short-sighted protest about the publication in 1964 by the Branch of Ann Westra's *Washday at the Pa*. This is a photographic study of life in a Maori village and a 38,000 copies edition had to be withdrawn following protests that the conditions shown were atypical. A commercial publisher could have faced the music—and probably achieved a best-seller. An official publisher could not. The book has since been republished by the Caxton Press.

No New Zealand children's book has yet achieved an international sale, or become widely known overseas (though a few, such as Stella Morice's *Wiremu*, have been reprinted in England) and a study of the Esther Glen awards suggests that, as with Canada, her writers for children are still in the stage of producing peripheral books and that no school of established fiction writers has yet emerged. Some books worth mention are Joyce West's *Year of the Shining Cuckoo*, Elsie Locke's *Runaway Settlers* and Anne de Roos's *Gold Dog*.

South Africa

South African children's books present a special difficulty, not only because South Africa is no longer a member of the Commonwealth but also because of the problem of language. English is only one of a number of official languages in South Africa. In some parts, like the Transkei, it is one of three official languages, the other two being Afrikaans and Xhosa; in South West Africa, again, it is one of three official languages—Afrikaans, German and English; in other parts of the country different native languages are used as one of the official languages. English is *spoken* in most parts of South Africa, but it is not the only official language, and cannot in any real sense be described as the language of the country.

Drawing by William Papas for Dark Waters, *by P. H. Nortje (Oxford University Press).*

Furthermore, although there are a few South African authors who write in English, the best known probably being Jenny Seed and Gwen Westwood, the majority of South African books for children are written in Afrikaans and can only be read in English in translation—when English translations are available—and there are a number of Afrikaans writers whose standard is locally considered to be higher than that of the few South African books written in English. Since I do not read Afrikaans I am not competent to assess such writers as Alba Bouwer, Freda Line and Hester Heese. P. H. Nortje's books, *The Green Ally*, *Wild Goose Summer* and *Dark Waters*, can however be read in English translations and these seem to support the South African assessment.

On a number of counts, therefore, it does not seem practicable to include here a worthwhile assessment of the South African contribution to children's books. The most important of these is the fact that it is no longer correct (if it ever was) to describe them as 'British' children's books. Many of them are written in Afrikaans and when translations are published they are as likely to be in German as in English. And since I cannot read Afrikaans other people's opinions would have to be accepted for a major part of the study and that is not a method that has been adopted elsewhere in this book.

South African children's books would undoubtedly make an interesting study, for the cross-fertilization of languages, cultures, and social backgrounds and the stresses of the contemporary political and racial situation must influence what is written for children. But anyone undertaking such a study would need to be multi-lingual, for he would need to be able to read fluently not only in English and Afrikaans but also in German to be able to arrive at a fair assessment of the relative merits of all authors who have written for children in South Africa.

Lydia Pienaar of the Cape Town City Libraries contributed an article in English on library work with children's books in South Africa to *Library Service for Children, Part II*, published by the International Federation of Library Associations (Committee on Library Work with Children) which is of interest on the language problem and the development of Afrikaans.

Other Commonwealth Countries

Although children's books written in English are now beginning to appear from other parts of the Commonwealth there are no other national schools of writing as yet. Andrew Salkey, a Jamaican now living in London, has written a number of books for children dealing with the disasters of which his own country seems to have more than its share, *Drought*, *Earthquake*, *Hurricane* and *Riot*; and C. Everard Palmer has also written children's books about life in the West Indies.

Carnegie Awards

Appendix B

Award Winners

When the first edition of this book was published in 1952 the Carnegie Medal was the only important award for British children's books. Annual awards had already been established in Australia and Canada but they had received little recognition. Most English-speaking countries now have such awards and, in addition, a British award for illustration has been founded, the Kate Greenaway Medal. There is usually controversy about any award winner, in any country. Opinions seem equally divided between those who consider that an award controlled solely by librarians is likely to produce a list of books that only librarians (and critics) read; and those who feel equally strongly that awards judged by 'well-meaning amateurs' are likely to result in ill-considered choices, or too popular a kind to be 'valuable' or to achieve the objects aimed at. What those objects are, or should be, remains open to doubt, but at least the reader can be certain that books which gain such awards are worthy of notice and likely to be, if no more, among the best of their kind published in the year. Such lists form, therefore, a useful starting point for the study of the books of any country.

The Carnegie Medal

The Carnegie Medal has been awarded annually (except in years when no book reached the standard set by the judges) since 1936. It was founded and is governed by the Library Association and was named in honour of Andrew Carnegie, to whose generosity the Association owes so much, in commemoration of the centenary of his birth, in 1935. The Carnegie Medal was originally awarded for what was, in the opinion of anonymous librarian judges, the most outstanding book of the year for children, written by a British subject, domiciled in the United Kingdom and published in Great Britain during the previous year. In 1969 the terms of the award were amended to include any 'outstanding book for children written in English and receiving its first publication in the United Kingdom during the preceding year', and also to make it possible for the same author to win the award more than once.

Anyone who has been responsible in any capacity for the administration of an award of this kind will appreciate the complications such a definition may introduce, but at least it removes the difficulty about books by Irish or Commonwealth authors—and makes it possible for the judges to make a good award in a bad year. That is, they need no longer strain to persuade themselves that a mediocre book is good enough because it is the best book by a 'new' author in that year, but can instead make a second award to some earlier winner.

Looking back at this list of 35 years of medal winners it is easy enough to criticise. The standards of the books chosen vary widely; not all seem first-class; there is a preponderance of fantasy, and so on. But such criticisms ignore the difficulties of judges faced with a single year's output of books. In a poor year a lesser book may win an award because it is just good enough and there is nothing better; in a good year there may be several obvious contenders—but only one can be chosen. (One can sympathise with the 1967 judges, faced as they were with a decision between such books as *Midway, The Piemakers, Flambards, Smith* and *The Owl Service*, any one of which could have been a winner in a lesser year.)

Furthermore, those who criticise the judges forget the astonishing difference between most of the pre-1950 books and those of later years. The first winner, Arthur Ransome with *Pigeon Post*, was beyond challenge and it must give everyone concerned lasting satisfaction that such outstanding work should have been the first to be recognised by the award. Then there was for a long time nothing of the same class. Walter De La Mare's *Collected Short Stories for Children* (though perhaps not quite what the award was aimed at) would have been remarkable in any company, but there was little else of the highest standard. Almost any of those early awards could be criticised. But from 1950 the position changed. From that date on, although it is still possible to argue about the choice in a given year, it would be carping criticism to argue that a bad book had been chosen. One might, in 1954, have preferred *The Children of Green Knowe* to *Knight Crusader*, or *A Swarm in May* to *The Little Bookroom* in 1955, but any of these books would have been worthy of the award and the list as a whole is a credit to the judges. From first to last there is little missing that an objective critic would expect to see in it and though some of the books chosen in the early years may not now be thought the best they seemed so in their day and were worthy of recognition.

1936 Arthur Ransome *Pigeon Post* (Cape)

1937 Eve Garnett *The Family From One End Street* (Muller)

1938 Noel Streatfeild *The Circus is Coming* (Dent)

1939 Eleanor Doorly *Radium Woman* (Heinemann)

1940 Kitty Barne *Visitors from London* (Dent)

1941 Mary Treadgold *We Couldn't Leave Dinah* (Cape)

1942 'B.B.' (D. J. Watkins-Pitchford) *The Little Grey Men* (Eyre and Spottiswoode)

1943 Prize withheld as no book considered suitable

1944 Eric Linklater *The Wind on the Moon* (Macmillan)

1945 Prize withheld as no book considered suitable

1946 Elizabeth Goudge *The Little White Horse* (Brockhampton Press, originally University of London Press)

1947 Walter De La Mare *Collected Short Stories for Children* (Faber)

1948 Richard Armstrong *Sea Change* (Dent)

1949 Agnes Allen *The Story of Your Home* (Faber)

1950 Elfrida Vipont *The Lark On The Wing* (Oxford University Press)

1951 Cynthia Harnett *The Wool-Pack* (Methuen)

1952 Mary Norton *The Borrowers* (Dent)

1953 Edward Osmond *A Valley Grows Up* (Oxford University Press)

1954 Ronald Welch *Knight Crusader* (Oxford University Press)

1955 Eleanor Farjeon *The Little Bookroom* (Oxford University Press)

1956 C. S. Lewis *The Last Battle* (The Bodley Head)

1957 William Mayne *A Grass Rope* (Oxford University Press)

1958 Philippa Pearce *Tom's Midnight Garden* (Oxford University Press)

1959 Rosemary Sutcliff *The Lantern Bearers* (Oxford University Press)

1960 I. W. Cornwall *The Making of Man* (Phoenix House)

1961 L. M. Boston *A Stranger at Green Knowe* (Faber)

1962 Pauline Clarke *The Twelve and the Genii* (Faber)

1963 Hester Burton *Time of Trial* (Oxford University Press)

1964 Sheena Porter *Nordy Bank* (Oxford University Press)

1965 Philip Turner *The Grange at High Force* (Oxford University Press)

1966 Prize withheld as no book considered suitable

1967 Alan Garner *The Owl Service* (Collins)

1968 Rosemary Harris *The Moon in the Cloud* (Faber)

1969 K. M. Peyton *The Edge of the Cloud* (Oxford University Press)

1970 Leon Garfield and Edward Blishen *The God Beneath The Sea* (Longman)

The Kate Greenaway Medal

The Kate Greenaway Medal was founded by the Library Association in 1955 to recognise the importance of illustration in children's books. It is awarded to the artist who, in the opinion of the Association, has produced the most distinguished work in the illustration of children's books published in the United Kingdom during the preceding year.

1955 Prize withheld as no book considered suitable

1956 Edward Ardizzone *Tim All Alone* (Oxford University Press)

1957 V. H. Drummond *Mrs Easter and the Storks* (Faber)

Appendix B. Award Winners

1958 Prize withheld as no book considered suitable

1959 William Stobbs *Kashtanka* and *A Bundle of Ballads* (Oxford University Press)

1960 Gerald Rose *Old Winkle and the Seagulls* (Faber)

1961 Antony Maitland *Mrs Cockle's Cat* (Longman, originally Constable)

1962 Brian Wildsmith *ABC* (Oxford University Press)

1963 John Burningham *Borka; The Adventures of a Goose with No Feathers* (Cape)

1964 C. Walter Hodges *Shakespeare's Theatre* (Oxford University Press)

1965 Victor Ambrus *The Three Poor Tailors* (Oxford University Press)

1966 Raymond Briggs *Mother Goose Treasury* (Hamish Hamilton)

1967 Charles Keeping *Charley, Charlotte and the Golden Canary* (Oxford University Press)

1968 Pauline Baynes *A Dictionary of Chivalry* (Longman)

1969 Helen Oxenbury *The Quangle Wangle's Hat* and *The Dragon of an Ordinary Family* (Heinemann)

1970 John Burningham *Mr Gumpy's Outing* (Cape)

The Australian Book of the Year Award

This award was originated by the Children's Book Council of New South Wales in 1946. In 1949 the Children's Book Councils of New South Wales and Victoria combined to make a joint award and in 1959 the award was taken over by the newly formed Australian Children's Book Council. The judges consist of a committee of six, one nominated by each State Children's Book Council, usually children's librarians. The Council's award is a bronze medal, but this has been supplemented in recent years by a grant of $500 to the winning author from the Australian Commonwealth Literary Fund.

1946 Leslie Rees *Karrawingi the Emu* (John Sands)

1947 No award

1948 Frank Hurley *Shackleton's Argonauts* (Angus and Robertson)

1949 Allan Villiers *Whalers of the Midnight Sun* (Angus and Robertson)

1950 No award

1951 Ruth C. Williams *Verity of Sydney Town* (Angus and Robertson)

1952 Eve Pownall *The Australia Book* (John Sands)

1953 Joan Phipson *Good Luck to the Rider* (Angus and Robertson) and J. D. and W. D. Martin *Aircraft of Today and Tomorrow* (Angus and Robertson)

1954 K. Langloh Parker *Australian Legendary Tales* (Angus and Robertson)

1955 Norman B. Tindall and H. A. Lindsay *The First Walkabout* (Longman)

1956 Patricia Wrightson *The Crooked Snake* (Angus and Robertson) and Peggy Barnard *Wish and the Magic Nut* (John Sands)

1957 Enid Moodie-Heddle *The Boomerang Book of Legendary Tales* (Longman)

1958 Nan Chauncy *Tiger in the Bush* (Oxford University Press)

1959 Nan Chauncy *Devil's Hill* (Oxford University Press) and John Gunn *Sea Menace* (Constable)

1960 Kylie Tennant *All the Proud Tribesmen* (Macmillan)

1961 Nan Chauncy *Tangara* (Oxford University Press)

1962 L. F. Evers *The Racketty Street Gang* (Hodder and Stoughton) and Joan Woodberry *Rafferty Rides A Winner* (Parrish)

1963 Joan Phipson *The Family Conspiracy* (Angus and Robertson)

1964 Eleanor Spence *The Green Laurel* (Oxford University Press)

1965 H. F. Brinsmead *Pastures of the Blue Crane* (Oxford University Press)

1966 Ivan Southall *Ash Road* (Angus and Robertson)

1967 Mavis T. Clark *The Min-Min* (Lansdowne)

1968 Ivan Southall *To The Wild Sky* (Angus and Robertson)

1969 Margaret Balderson *When Jays Fly to Barbmo* (Oxford University Press)

1970 Annette MacArthur-Onslow *Uhu* (Ure Smith)

Appendix B. Award Winners

The Esther Glen Award

This award was established in 1945 for the best children's book published in New Zealand each year. It was founded by the New Zealand Library Association to encourage writing of quality in New Zealand children's literature and awards are made only 'to books of distinct merit'. The award is named in honour of Esther Glen, an author of New Zealand stories and verse for children, most of whose writing was done early in this century. Although the award can be made annually only five books have so far been honoured.

1945 Stella M. Morice *The Book of Wiremu* (Progressive Publishing Society)
1947 Alexander W. Reed *Myths and Legends of Maoriland* (Reed)
1950 John Smith *The Adventures of Nimble, Rumble and Tumble* (Paul)
1959 Maurice N. Duggan *Falter Tom and the Water Boy* (Paul)
1964 Lesley C. Powell *Turi, the Story of a little boy* (Paul)

The Canadian Book of the Year Award

This award, in the form of a bronze medal, is presented by the Canadian Association of Children's Librarians for the best children's book by a Canadian author. For several years the award was given two years after the date of publication and in 1966 there were two awards in the same year because of a change in the award procedure.

1947 Roderick L. Haig-Brown *Starbuck Valley Winter* (Morrow)
1948 Mabel Dunham *Kristli's Trees* (McClelland and Stewart)
1949 No award
1950 Richard S. Lambert *Franklin of the Arctic* (McClelland and Stewart)
1951 No award
1952 Catherine Anthony Clark *The Sun Horse* (Macmillan)

183

1953–1955 No award

1956 Louise Riley *Train for Tiger Lily* (Macmillan)

1957 Cyrus Macmillan *Glooskap's Country and Other Indian Tales* (Oxford University Press)

1958 Farley Mowat *Lost in the Barrens* (Little, Brown)

1959 John F. Hayes *The Dangerous Cove* (Copp, Clark)

1960 Marius Barbeau *The Golden Phoenix* (Oxford University Press)

1961 William Toye *The St Lawrence* (Oxford University Press)

1962 No award

1963 Sheila Burnford *The Incredible Journey* (Little, Brown)

1964 Roderick L. Haig-Brown *The Whale People* (Collins)

1965 Dorothy M. Reid *Tales of Nanabozho* (Oxford University Press)

1966 James McNeill *The Double Knights* (Oxford University Press) and James Houston *Tikta'Liktak* (Longman)

1967 Christie Harris *Raven's Cry* (McClelland and Stewart)

1968 Kay Hill *Tomorrow The Stars* (Dodd Mead)

1969 Edith Fowke *Sally Go Round The Sun* (McClelland and Stewart)

1970 William Toye *Cartier Discovers the St Lawrence* (Oxford University Press)

The Arts Council Award

In 1969 the Arts Council for the first time made two awards specifically for children's books. The awards covered books published between 1966 and 1968, and were given to *The Green Children*, by Kevin Crossley-Holland and Margaret Gordon (Macmillan), as the best book for younger children, and to *Smith*, by Leon Garfield (Longman), as the best book for older children.

The Guardian *Award*

In 1967 *The Guardian* announced an annual award of one hundred guineas for an outstanding contribution to children's literature. The winner is chosen by a panel of *Guardian* reviewers under the chairmanship of the children's books editor.

1967 Leon Garfield *Devil-in-the-Fog* (Longman, originally Constable)
1968 Alan Garner *The Owl Service* (Collins)
1969 Joan Aiken *The Whispering Mountain* (Cape)
1970 K. M. Peyton The *Flambards* trilogy (Oxford University Press)
1971 John Christopher *The Guardians* (Hamish Hamilton)

The Eleanor Farjeon Award

This award was founded in 1965 by the Children's Book Circle in honour of Eleanor Farjeon. It is awarded for a significant contribution in relation to children's books and reading in the preceding year. The Children's Book Circle is an informal group of men and women working in the children's editorial departments of publishing firms.

1965 Margery Fisher
1966 Jessica Jenkins
1967 Brian Alderson
1968 Anne Wood
1969 Kaye Webb
1970 Margaret Meek

Appendix C

A Select Bibliography of Books about Children's Books

Although children's books are now studied more widely and in greater depth than they were in 1950, the literature is still not extensive. Much of it is also still American and therefore of less value to readers of the present work than the smaller— but qualitatively high—British contribution. Only in one or two special cases therefore have books originating on the other side of the Atlantic been included in this select list.

The purpose of the list is twofold: first, to distinguish the different categories into which information about English children's books may be divided, and second, to show the way in which writing in the various categories has developed. Just as children's books themselves have increased in the last twenty years, so the literature about them has, and by listing this literature chronologically within each category it is hoped that a faint pattern of the history of the study of children's literature will emerge.

While annotations have been added in order to assist clarity, no extensive effort has been made to describe or evaluate the material listed here. In selecting the books I have tried to include only those that seem to me to have value for the reader who wishes to take the first steps in exploring territory which is not widely known. Fuller information about more detailed books and articles on the subject may be found in the items listed in Section I.

For those readers uncertain how to approach the books

listed here I should like to suggest that John Rowe Townsend's *Written For Children* (in Section IIa) will make an entertaining and thought-provoking introduction to the history of imaginative literature for children, and that Margery Fisher's *Intent Upon Reading* (in Section III) forms a natural follow-on to the introductory discussions of twentieth-century trends that I have attempted here.

Section I: Bibliographies

F. W. BATESON (editor) *The Cambridge Bibliography of English Literature*. Cambridge University Press, 1940.
This major work in four volumes, with a supplement published in 1957, is a descendant of *The Cambridge History of English Literature*, whose bibliographies provided it with a starting point. Extensive lists on children's literature appear in volumes 2 and 3, both compiled by F. J. Harvey Darton, who contributed the essays on the subject to the original *History*. A completely new edition of the *Bibliography* is now in preparation under the editorship of George Watson. Volume 3 on the nineteenth century was published in 1970, and a completely new volume on the twentieth century, which will include coverage of children's books, is scheduled for publication in 1972 or 1973.

FRANK EYRE *Notes for a Bibliography* in *Junior Bookshelf*, 16, 1952.

MARCUS CROUCH *Books about Children's Literature*. Library Association (1963), 2nd edition 1966.

VIRGINIA HAVILAND (editor) *Children's Literature: a Guide to Reference Sources*. Washington, Library of Congress, 1966.
Prepared on behalf of the Children's Services Division of the Library of Congress, this volume represents the fullest attempt yet to list and describe books and periodical articles on both English and American children's literature.

Section II: History

(a) General and Special Studies

CHARLES WELSH *A Bookseller of the Last Century (John Newbery)*. Griffith, Farran, 1885.

CHARLES WELSH *On Some of the Books for Children of the Last Century*. London, Privately Printed, 1886.

LOUISE FRANCES FIELD *The Child and His Book*. Wells Gardner, Darton, 1891.

Appendix C. A Select Bibliography

E. S. HARTLAND *The Science of Fairy Tales*. W. Scott, 1891.

ANDREW TUER *History of the Horn Book*. Leadenhall Press, 1896.

LINA ECKENSTEIN *Comparative Studies of Nursery Rhymes*. Duckworth, 1906.

FLORENCE V. BARRY *A Century of Children's Books*. Methuen, 1922.
A study of eighteenth-century books.

F. J. HARVEY DARTON *Children's Books in England: five centuries of social life*. Cambridge University Press (1932), 2nd edition, revised by Kathleen Lines, 1958.

PAUL HAZARD *Books, Children and Men*. Boston, The Horn Book Inc., 1944.
One of the few books that try to trace some of the international relationships in the field of children's books.

ROGER LANCELYN GREEN *Tellers of Tales*. Edmund Ward (1946), rewritten and revised edition, 1969.
First published as a book for children, this work has been converted into an introductory survey for the interested adult.

IONA AND PETER OPIE *The Oxford Dictionary of Nursery Rhymes*. Oxford, Clarendon Press, 1951.

PERCY MUIR *English Children's Books*, 1600–1900. Batsford, 1954.

E. S. TURNER *Boys Will Be Boys*. Michael Joseph (1948), 2nd edition, 1957.

M. F. THWAITE *From Primer to Pleasure: an Introduction to the History of Children's Books in England*. Library Association, 1963.

GILLIAN AVERY, with ANGELA BULL *Nineteenth-century children: heroes and heroines in English children's stories*. Hodder and Stoughton, 1965.

JOHN ROWE TOWNSEND *Written for Children: an outline of English Children's Literature*. Garnet Miller, 1965.

BETTINA HURLIMANN *Three Centuries of Children's Books in Europe*. Oxford University Press, 1967.

(b) Edited Facsimiles of Early Children's Books

JOHN ASHTON *Chapbooks of the Eighteenth Century*. Chatto and Windus, 1882.
Itself reproduced in facsimile, with an introduction by Victor Neuburg, Welwyn Garden City, Seven Dials Press, 1969.

ANDREW TUER *Pages and Pictures from Forgotten Children's Books*. Leadenhall Press, 1898.

ANDREW TUER *Stories from Old Fashioned Children's Books*. Leadenhall Press, 1899; reprinted by Evelyn, Adams and McKay, 1969.

LEONARD DE VRIES *Flowers of Delight*. Dobson, 1965.

M. F. THWAITE *A Little Pretty Pocket-Book.* Oxford University Press, 1966.

LEONARD DE VRIES *Little Wide Awake.* Arthur Barker, 1967.

JILL E. GREY *The Governess.* Oxford University Press, 1968.

VICTOR E. NEUBURG *The Penny Histories.* Oxford University Press, 1968.

J. H. P. PAFFORD *Divine Songs Attempted in Easy Language for the Use of Children.* Oxford University Press, 1971.

(c) Catalogues of Collections, Exhibitions, etc.

NATIONAL BOOK LEAGUE *Children's Books of Yesterday.* National Book League, 1948.

EDGAR OSBORNE *From Morality and Instruction to Beatrix Potter.* Eastbourne Corporation, 1949.

JUDITH ST JOHN (editor) *The Osborne Collection of Early Children's Books,* 1566–1910. Toronto Public Library, 1958.

M. F. THWAITE (editor) *Children's Books of this Century.* Library Association, Youth Libraries Section, 1958.
A collection being formed as 'an attempt to record some of the more important books and trends in publishing for children in this century'.

BRITISH MUSEUM *An Exhibition of Early Children's Books.* British Museum, 1968.

Section III: Guides and Critical Discussions of Twentieth-century Children's Books

MAY LAMBERTON BECKER *Choosing Books for Children.* Oxford University Press, 1937.
The English version, edited and with British books substituted, of *First Adventures in Reading,* published in the United States in 1936.

DOROTHY NEAL WHITE *About Books for Children.* Oxford University Press, 1946.

GEOFFREY TREASE *Tales Out Of School.* Heinemann (1948); 2nd edition, 1964.

GEOFFREY TREASE *Enjoying Books.* Phoenix House, 1951.
A survey intended for children.

DOROTHY NEAL WHITE *Books Before Five.* New Zealand Council for Educational Research, 1954.

MARCUS CROUCH *Chosen for Children: an Account of the Books Which Have Been Awarded the Library Association Carnegie Medal, 1936–1957.* Library Association (1957); revised edition, 1967.

Appendix C. A Select Bibliography

BORIS FORD (editor) *Young Writers, Young Readers*. Hutchinson, 1960.
Examples of the way children write, and a critical discussion of some of the books they read.

MARGERY FISHER *Intent Upon Reading: a Critical Appraisal of Modern Fiction for Children*. Brockhampton Press (1961); 2nd edition, 1964.

MARCUS CROUCH *Treasure Seekers and Borrowers: Children's Books in Britain, 1900–1960*. Library Association (1961); amended edition, 1970.

AIDAN CHAMBERS *The Reluctant Reader*. Pergamon Press, 1969.

SHEILA EGOFF, G. T. STUBBS and L. F. ASHLEY (editors) *Only Connect*. Oxford University Press, 1969.
A collection of papers on children's writing, covering an exceptionally wide range and including many memorable pieces.

WALLACE HILDICK *Children and Fiction*. Evans, 1970.

JOHN ROWE TOWNSEND *A Sense of Story: Essays on Contemporary Writers for Children*. Longman, 1971.

Section IV: Surveys

A. J. JENKINSON *What Do Boys and Girls Read?* Methuen (1940); revised edition, 1946.

W. J. SCOTT *Reading, Film and Radio Tastes of High School Girls and Boys*. Oxford University Press, 1947.

GEORGE NORVELL *The Reading Interests of Young People*. D. C. Heath, 1950.

I. J. LENG *Children in Libraries*. University of Wales Press, 1968.

PETER H. MANN and JACQUELINE L. BURGOYNE *Books and Reading*. André Deutsch, 1969.
The first report of an inquiry into 'the sociology of reading' sponsored by the Charter Group of the Booksellers Association. Chapter 2, by Miss Burgoyne, discusses 'Growing Into Reading'.

Section V: Book Lists

LIBRARY ASSOCIATION *Books for Youth*. Library Association, 1926.
Followed in 1930 by *Books to Read*, which was given a first supplement in 1931.

LILLIAN H. SMITH (editor) *Books for Boys and Girls*. Toronto, The Ryerson Press, 1927.
An authoritative list later revised and supplemented by Jean Thomson through several editions.

Appendix C. A Select Bibliography

KATHLEEN LINES *Books for Young People*. National Book Council, 1937.
Revised, extended and issued a year later under the title *Four to Fourteen*, a list now recognised as of seminal importance in establishing standards for book selection. Revised editions appeared in 1950 and 1956, the publisher by then having changed its name to the National Book League.

J. G. FARADAY *Twelve Years of Children's Books*. Cambridge, 1939.

MURIEL STEEL *Books You'll Enjoy*. Grafton, 1939.

DOROTHY M. NEAL *Junior Books: a Recommended List for Boys and Girls*. New Zealand Library Association, 1940.

A. A. MILNE *Books for Children: a Reader's Guide*. National Book League, 1948.

SUNDAY TIMES *The One Hundred Best Books for Children*. Sunday Times, 1958.

OSBORNE, C. H. C. (editor) *Primary School Library Books: an annotated list*. School Library Association (1960); 2nd edition by F. Sturt, 1965; 3rd edition, as *Books for Primary Children*, by B. Clark, 1969.
An example of the thorough lists compiled by this Association since its formation in 1937. Other lists relate more closely to non-fiction publications.

NATIONAL BOOK LEAGUE *British Children's Books*. National Book League, 1964.
An important retrospective list of the century's children's books, a further edition having been published in 1967. Apart from such lists as this and *Four to Fourteen*, the League has been responsible for issuing many smaller lists for specific purposes, often associated with its travelling exhibitions.

NAOMI LEWIS *The Best Children's Books of 1963*. Hamish Hamilton, 1964.
An annual review, further volumes of which cover the years 1964–1967.

NANCY CHAMBERS (editor) *Reading for Enjoyment*. Children's Booknews, 1970.
A set of four descriptive lists prepared for different age groupings and compiled by Brian Alderson, Aidan Chambers, Jessica Jenkins and Elaine Moss.

Section VI: Special Topics

(a) Storytelling

MARIE L. SHEDLOCK *The Art of the Story-Teller*. 3rd edition, New York, Dover, 1952.
Originally published in 1915 as *The Art of Story-Telling*.

Appendix C. A Select Bibliography

ELIZABETH CLARK *Stories To Tell and How To Tell Them*. University of London Press, 1917.

WOUTRINA A. BONE *Children's Stories and How To Tell Them*. Christophers, 1924.

ARTHUR BURRELL *A Guide to Story Telling*. Isaac Pitman, 1926.

RUTH SAWYER *The Way of the Storyteller*. New York, Viking (1942); 2nd edition, 1962. Published in England by the Bodley Head, 1966.

EILEEN COLWELL (editor) *A Storyteller's Choice*. The Bodley Head, 1963.
First of a carefully compiled series of anthologies, which include notes to the storyteller.

ELIZABETH COOK *The Ordinary and the Fabulous: an Introduction to Myths, Legends and Fairy Tales for Teachers and Storytellers*. Cambridge University Press, 1969.

ANTHONY JONES and JUNE BUTTREY *Children and Stories*. Blackwell, 1970.

(b) Illustration

CHARLES WELSH *On Coloured Books for Children*. Wyman, 1887.

GLEESON WHITE *Children's Books and their Illustrators* in *The Studio* (winter number), 1898.

PHILIP JAMES *Children's Books of Yesterday* in *The Studio* (autumn number), 1933.

PHILIP JAMES *English Book Illustration, 1800–1900*. Penguin, 1947.

JANET ADAM SMITH *Children's Illustrated Books*. Collins, 1948.

DAVID BLAND *The Illustration of Books*. Faber (1951); 3rd edition, 1962.
Contains a chapter on children's books, references to which will also be found in the same author's exhaustive *History of Book Illustration*, Faber, 2nd edition, 1969.

CHARLES H. MORRIS *The Illustration of Children's Books*. Library Association, 1957.

JOHN RYDER *Artists of a Certain Line*. The Bodley Head, 1960.

LYNTON LAMB *Drawing for Illustration*. Oxford University Press, 1962.

DAVID THOMAS *Children's Book Illustration in England* in *The Penrose Annual*, vol. 56, Lund Humphries, 1962.

ROBIN JACQUES *Illustrators at Work*. Studio, 1963.

(c) Children's Books in the Commonwealth

ROSEMARY WIGHTON *Early Australian Children's Literature*. Oxford University Press, 1963.

NEW ZEALAND NATIONAL LIBRARY SERVICE *Books about New Zealand*. Wellington, New Zealand National Library Service, 1964.

HUGH ANDERSON *The Singing Roads.* Wentworth, 1965.
Biographies of Australian writers.

SHEILA EGOFF *The Republic of Childhood.* Oxford University Press, 1967.
A study of Canadian children's literature.

MAURICE SAXBY *A History of Australian Children's Literature.* Wentworth, 1969.

CHILDREN'S BOOK COUNCIL OF VICTORIA *Australian Children's Books: A Select List.* Melbourne, Children's Book Council of Victoria, 1970.

MARCIE MUIR *A Bibliography of Australian Children's Books.* André Deutsch, 1970.

Section VIII: Periodicals

Junior Bookshelf. Huddersfield, 1936–   .
Published six times a year. Edited by Diana Morrell.

The School Librarian. School Library Association, 1937–   .
Originally published three times a year, quarterly from 1969. The journal is currently edited by Norman Furlong, the reviews by Margaret Meek.

Times Literary Supplement. Times Newspapers, 1902–   . From 1949 there have been two, from 1968 four special issues a year devoted to children's books.

Growing Point. Northampton, 1962–   .
Edited Margery Fisher. Published nine times a year.

Children's Book News. Children's Booknews Ltd., 1964–1970.
Published six times a year. Edited for part of its brief span by Nancy Chambers and, later, Valerie Alderson.

Books For Your Children. Aldershot, 1965–   .
Published quarterly. Edited by Anne Wood.

Children's Literature in Education. Ward Lock Educational, 1970–   .
Published three times a year. Edited by a panel of educationists centred on St Luke's College of Education, Exeter.

Signal: Approaches to Children's Literature. Stroud, The Thimble Press, 1970–   .
Published three times a year. Edited by Nancy Chambers.

Children's Book Review. Wormley, Herts., The Five Owls Press, 1971–   .
Published six times a year. Edited by Valerie Alderson.

In addition to these specialist journals, articles about and reviews of children's books have occurred with growing frequency in daily newspapers, such as *The Daily Telegraph, The Guardian* and *The Times,* in Sunday papers, such as *The Observer* and *The Sunday*

Times, in the 'cultural weeklies' such as *The New Statesman* and *The Spectator*, and in various specialist education and library
Times, in the 'cultural weeklies' such as The *New Statesman* and The *Spectator*, and in various specialist education and library periodicals.

Section IX: Biographical Works

Information about the authors of children's books is to be found in sources too many and too various to be listed here; standard biographies, biographical reference works, autobiographies, journals, short studies, such as the series of Bodley Head *Monographs*, and, indeed, in many works devoted to the history of literature. Initial guidance to the range of works may be gained from Marcus Crouch's *Books About Children's Literature*, noted in Section I, and from the bibliography to Brian Doyle's *Who's Who of Children's Literature*, Evelyn, 1968.

Section X: Library Work with Children's Books

W. C. BERWICK SAYERS *A Manual of Children's Libraries*. Allen and Unwin, 1932.

A Guide for School Librarians. Oxford University Press, 1937.

Model School Library Shelf-List. Public Library of New South Wales, 1937.

C. A. STOTT *School Libraries: A Short Manual*. Cambridge University Press, 1947.

R. G. RALPH *The Library in Education*. Phoenix House, 1949.

E. GRIMSHAW *The Teacher Librarian*. Edward Arnold, 1952.

L. R. COLVIN *Public Library Service for Children*. Unesco, 1957.

J. A. CUTFORTH *Children and Books*. Basil Blackwell, 1962.

R. O. LINDEN *Books and Libraries*. Cassell, 1965.

ERNEST ROE *Teachers, Librarians and Children*. Crosby Lockwood, 1965.

S. I. FENWICK *School and Children's Libraries in Australia*. Cheshire, 1966.

MELVYN BARNES *Youth Library Work*. Clive Bingley, 1969.

Index

Index

Index

Index

Index

Index